# EFFECTIVE TEACHING AND LEARNING IN THE PRIMARY CLASSROOM

Sara Shaw and Trevor Hawes

This edition published in Great Britain in 1998 by
The SERVICES Ltd
P.O. Box 12
Leicester LE2 5AE
Telephone: 0116 2717217 Fax: 0116 2717219



ISBN 0 953 3531 0 9

Designed and typeset by Jane Barker.

Printed by Graphic Repro, Nottingham.

# CONTENTS

# PREFACE

## Why we wrote this book

The exciting advances neuro-scientists have made in increasing understanding of the human brain hold so many important messages for teachers. Not only is this information of enormous practical use in the classroom, but our experience of running 1 day courses has shown that it has a most invigorating effect on teachers themselves. Typically participants end the day with renewed enthusiasm and a high level of motivation. Teachers have found that our courses confirm best practice and strengthen confidence in their teaching skills – with new understandings of how to achieve best practice more of the time. They also take away some new techniques to maximise the effectiveness of their teaching.

This book, the first to target the material specifically at primary school teachers, has been written so that more teachers can benefit from this important information. We would like to thank the many Leicestershire schools whose enthusiastic response to our courses inspired us to go into print.

## Acknowledgements

We have drawn from the work of many who have made fundamentally important contributions to this field: we wish to acknowledge fully those contributions. In particular: Gordon Dryden and Jean Vos 'The Learning Revolution', Colin Rose 'Accelerated Learning', Eric Jensen's many books on the subject of Brain Compatible Learning, Howard Gardner 'Frames of Mind', Launa Ellison 'Seeing with Magic Glasses', Tony Buzan 'Use Your Head', Jane Healy 'Your Child's Growing Mind', Alistair Smith 'Accelerated Learning in the Classroom', Robert Dilts and Todd Epstein 'Dynamic Learning', Carla Hannaford 'Smart Moves', Daniel Goleman 'Emotional Intelligence'.

This book also draws much from the field of NLP (neuro-linguistic programming) which was developed by Dr Richard Bandler and Dr John Grinder and has much to offer teachers, particularly in the field of communication. Sara Shaw has trained as a MasterPractitioner through Dr Bandler and the Society of NLP (Centre NLP, Leicester) and wishes to acknowledge the significant contribution that training has made to this book.

Sara Shaw and Trevor Hawes

# INTRODUCTION

Over 80 per cent of what we understand about how the human brain functions has been learnt in the last 10 years. Neuro-scientists are now able to use PET and MRI scanners to watch the biological organ we call the brain at work and to identify how it learns and remembers.

This book draws upon the latest understanding of how the human brain operates and considers the implications this has for primary teachers and how they facilitate learning in the primary classroom.

In many ways the findings of the neuro-scientists support what is commonly understood to be "effective teaching" methods. The important contribution this research is making is to explain why particular teaching methods work so well. Our experience has been that, equipped with this information, teachers are able to achieve "best practice" more of the time and with more of their pupils.

The Labour Government has recognised the benefits that can result from the application of neuro-scientific research. In "Excellence in Schools" the Government states….."We will explore effective new approaches to teaching and learning and spread them across schools. We want to see more examples of accelerated learning based on the latest understanding of how people learn, which has enabled groups of students to progress at greater speed and with deeper understanding".

In "Effective Teaching and Learning in the Primary Classroom" we present the information that is of most relevance to Primary Teachers in their quest to optimise the quality and rate of learning that is achieved in their classrooms.

The first ten chapters of the book each focus on a particular aspect of learning. Each chapter starts with a summary diagram and concludes by considering the implications for classroom practice after which the reader is invited to draw up an action plan based upon what they have learned. The final chapter draws together the themes of the book and presents a strategy for optimising learning.

# CHAPTER ONE
# THE AMAZING HUMAN BRAIN

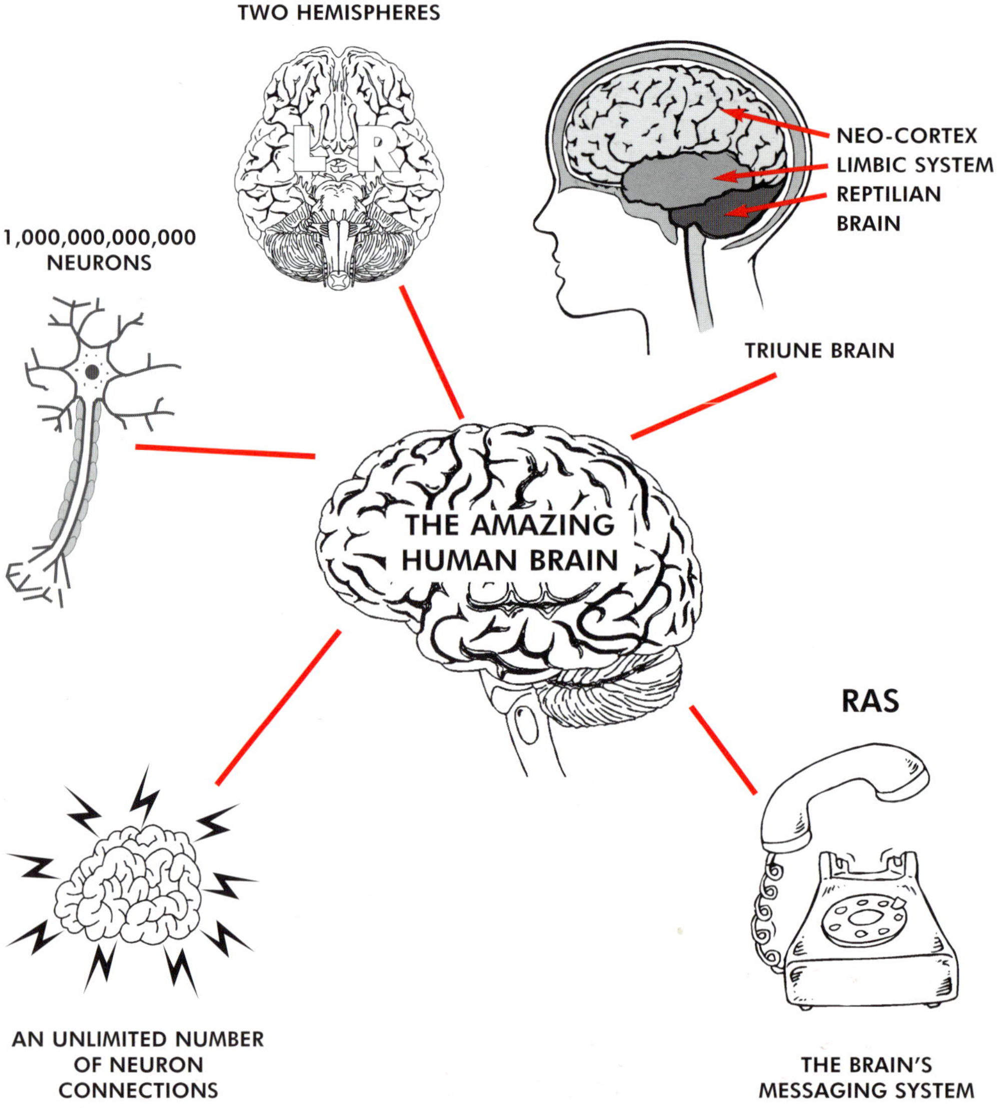

## THE AMAZING HUMAN BRAIN

Have you ever wished you could see inside your pupils' heads? That you could find out just what makes them tick, how their minds work, how best to get through to them?

The good news for all teachers is that the exciting breakthroughs made in recent years by neuro-scientists mean that it is now possible to write a basic instruction manual for the brain and how it learns. X-ray eyes may be some way into the future, but the light thrown by neuro-scientific research illuminates some fascinating paths for teachers to travel.

Equipped with these discoveries, primary school teachers can have a new understanding of best practice. We know that some teaching techniques seem to work well - now we can see why. We can set a direction in which to develop useful practices, and take a fresh look at those which may be less than useful.

A child's brain is not a miniature version of an adult's. In the course of a primary school education, many stages of development are passed through. Understanding that development gives many fresh insights into providing the sort of teaching and learning opportunities which will have the most effective results.

The following chapter studies the nature of human brain, in terms of the current understanding which seems to offer useful concepts for primary school practice. These include:

- the biological process which we know as learning
- the developmental sequence which takes a child from birth to adulthood
- the way in which the brain is structured as the survival organ of the human body.

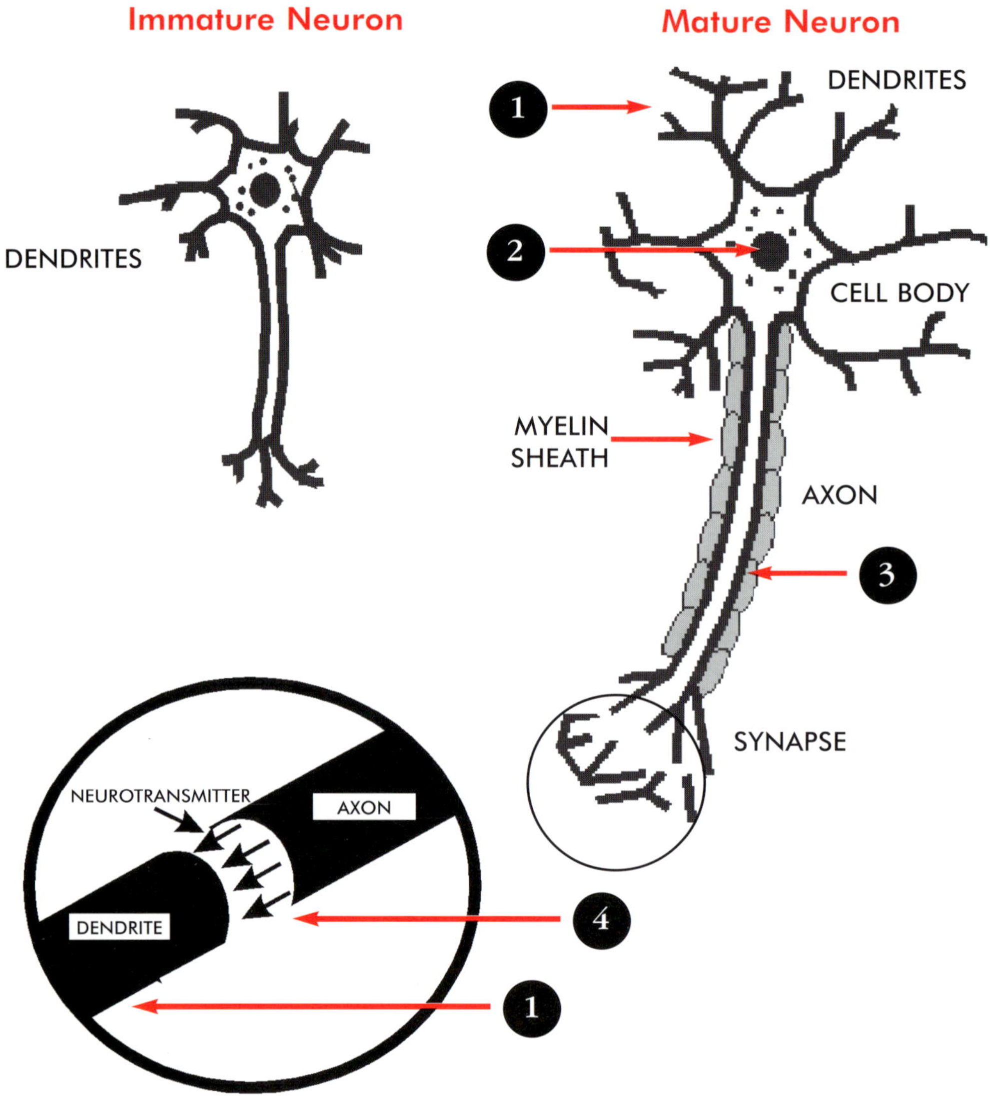


❶ Dendrite senses arrival of (chemical) neurotransmitters and passes electrical current to cell body.

❷ Cell body fires and;

❸ passes electrical current along axon.

❹ Neurotransmitters released - 'ferrying' message across the synaptic.

# THE RAW MATERIAL - WIRING UP THE BRAIN

One of the most exciting things that research has discovered is that the potential for developing our brain is almost unlimited, and by engaging in mentally stimulating activities we can keep expanding it even into old age.

Brain cells start to grow soon after conception, and in the course of the next nine months will be produced in their billions. During this time the physical structure of the brain begins to form as the learning cells or **neurons** travel to different areas and start to form systems and sub-systems, supported by the glial cells which feed and protect the neurons. This physical structure is often referred to as 'hard wiring'.

The new baby is born with a brain that is partially hard wired, but also with many 'spare' neurons, available for development. This is known as plasticity. Each individual then continues to wire up their brain according to their genetic inheritance and their environmental experience. A unique process, leading to a unique brain for every person.

The wiring up of the brain - the biological basis of learning - is the process by which systems of neurons connect up to each other, and form channels of communication through which messages can be electrically transmitted. This is a two part process, both parts of which have important implications for teachers:

## 1. Making connections

Stimulation via the senses causes certain neurons to connect up, and pass a message in the form of an electro/chemical impulse from one cell to another. Each neuron is equipped with a single transmitting arm (called the **axon**) and, in response to stimulation, can grow many branch-like receivers (called **dendrites**). The axon and dendrites grow to various lengths to "connect up". There is always a small gap between the transmitting axon and the receiving dendrite known as the "**synaptic gap**". A message starts as an electrical charge in the neuron cell body. The electricity runs down the axon and at the synapse stimulates the release of a chemical (known as a **neurotransmitter**) which "ferries" the message across the synaptic gap. The message is received by the dendrite of the connecting neuron, passing as electricity down to the cell's body for possible forward transmission to a connecting neuron.

## THE EVOLUTION OF THE HUMAN BRAIN

The human brain is primarily designed for survival, not learning, but has an awesome capacity to learn.

The human brain is the result of millions of years of evolution. Its primary function is to ensure the survival of the species.

It has a phenomenal capacity to learn and, providing techniques are used which are compatible with its survival-orientated processes, it can learn swiftly and recall effectively.

## THE BRAIN AND ENRICHMENT

American neuro-scientist Dr. Marion Diamond has conducted a series of experiments which prove that rats provided with a varied and stimulating environment grow heavier brains with more neural connections than those in an impoverished environment. Studies of children suggest that mental stimulation has a lasting effect in increasing intelligence.

What measures do you and your school take to provide an enriched environment?

Every time sensory stimulation occurs, dendrites reach out towards neighbouring axons to pick up the signal, growing longer and thicker in the process and narrowing the gap between them - thus facilitating effective connections. Communication becomes quicker and easier.

Connections between neurons are the basis of learning. Connections are created every time the child acts on stimulation of the senses through the environment. It is thought that an enriched environment offering a wide variety of sensory stimuli will greatly enhance learning. The more the brain learns, the more it becomes capable of learning.

It is much easier to build up existing neuron networks than to create new ones in isolation. Therefore, teaching which connects to previous knowledge, skills and understanding will be the most effective. This of course confirms what is already recognised as good practice - the use of ongoing formative assessment to ascertain a child's current position and build on it, using differentiation to ensure that each individual is taught at an appropriate level.

## 2. Myelination

As neurons make connections with each other they form pathways which develop into more and more complex systems. The next part of the process involves a covering of **myelin** along the pathways - a bit like the insulation on an electric cable. The **myelin sheath** helps to direct and conduct the message through the system. It is the finishing touch to the developing brain.

It takes a long time to myelinate a whole brain - into adulthood and beyond. Almost all myelination occurs after birth - starting with the lower brain and the motor functions such as walking, and progressing to the higher levels including abstract thought and reasoning. The sequence follows a certain order, but the speed varies among individuals - there is a normal development range of 18 months.

# "WHEN THE NEURONS ARE FIRING, THE BRAIN'S HARD WIRING"

Pat Wolfe

Until an area of the brain is myelinated, it is not fully developed. It may be futile therefore, or even damaging, to expect a child to perform learning tasks they are not yet biologically equipped for. One of the most fascinating facts learned about this process is that the sequence in which myelination takes place more or less corresponds to Piaget's stages of development.

Another enlightening fact is that the speed of myelination is influenced by gender. Boys, by reason of muscle density and hormone profiles, take longer to achieve myelination than girls. This means that many girls are myelinating the speech and language areas of their brains before their male counterparts. An answer perhaps to gender related patterns in learning to read (see pages 64-67).

## The Brain's Potential

If learning is the process of neurons making connections, how many of these connections is the average brain able to make? The answer to this appears to be that the number is so great as to be virtually unlimited - in fact so great that estimates of how much of our brain's potential we actually use, range from 1% - 4%!

In spite of the fact that our brain cells naturally die off from birth onwards, and are never replaced, we are so generously endowed with neurons that this loss is insignificant. What is important is the extent to which we stimulate and use our brains.

Just as a muscle which is used and exercised becomes fit and strong, and one which is unused gradually wastes away, an active brain continues growing by stimulating new connections.

An enriched environment will undoubtedly encourage children's brains to learn and develop, just as experiments have shown is the case for rats. Enrichment is likely to involve a wide provision for children to engage all their senses, rather than a hot house approach to skill acquisition without regard for developmental readiness.

# THE TRIUNE BRAIN

## Three brains in one

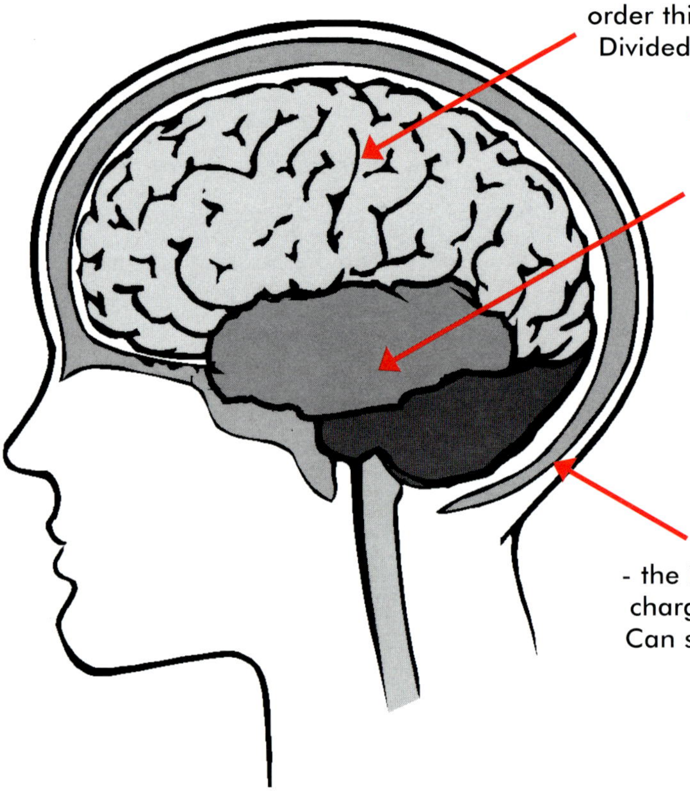

### The Neo-cortex

- the academic brain where higher order thinking skills take place. Divided into two hemsipheres.

### The Limbic System

- seat of the emotions and the sense of self identity and values. Regulates long term memory and attention.

### Reptilian brain

- the instinctive brain, taking charge of survival functions. Can shut down higher order thinking under stress.

# THE STRUCTURE OF THE BRAIN

The way in which the brain is organised - its physical structure - provides much interesting information for the teacher intent on providing the most effective learning environment within their classroom.

A ground-breaking model was proposed by Doctor Paul MacLean - known as Triune Brain theory - which has many implications for teaching and learning.

## The Triune Brain - Three Brains in One

Dr Paul MacLean of the National Institute of Mental Health, Washington DC, developed a theory about the human brain which suggests that it is a triune brain, made up of three distinct areas.

He named the three areas:-

- The Neo-cortex
- The Limbic System (or mid-brain), and
- The Reptilian Brain

The ***reptilian brain*** is at the base of the brain, and MacLean suggests that this is the oldest evolutionary part of the brain. The main responsibility of the reptilian brain is to ensure survival including controlling all routine body functions and instinctive behaviour.

The ***limbic system***, or ***mid-brain*** area deals with the emotions, belief and value systems, and long term memory.

The ***neo-cortex*** is seated at the top of the brain. This is the cognitive or thinking area. It is split into two hemispheres, joined by the corpus callosum. Thought to have evolved most recently, this part of the brain is the problem-solving and pattern seeking area.

# KEEPING THE REPTILIAN BRAIN HAPPY

## Things that make the reptilian brain happy

- The reptilian brain likes to have its own territorial space (named peg, drawer etc.)
- The reptilian brain needs physical comfort (warmth, light, absence of hunger and thirst etc.)
- The reptilian brain needs to belong, and enjoys rituals which confirm identity (allocated job, opening and closing rituals etc)
- The reptilian brain likes to feel safe, both physically and emotionally - reducing anxiety enhances learning.

## Ways of reducing anxiety:-

- Be clear about what you expect from children and what they can expect from you
- Praise five times as often as you criticise
- Criticise the behaviour not the child
- Be fair and consistent
- Avoid sarcasm and derogatory remarks
- Provide opportunities to talk about feelings and how to manage them
- Teach skills in dealing with peer group disputes
- Listen

## THE REPTILIAN BRAIN

The reptilian brain is responsible for routine body functions which operate continually outside our conscious awareness - such as breathing, heart beat, blood pressure, temperature, balance, etc.

It also takes charge of survival responses - e.g. the "fight or flight" response in the face of danger.

Certain instinctive behaviour still persists in the human being - adults and children - including a predisposition towards social conformity including hierarchies and 'pecking order'. We also respond to rote and ritual, another function of the reptilian brain.

The most important task for any individual or species is to ensure survival, and the brain is first and foremost a survival-orientated organ. In any potentially threatening situation, whether physical, emotional or psychological, the reptilian area takes precedence over the other two. Higher order functions such as learning take a back seat if the reptilian brain perceives any form of threat.

Understanding this leads us to a crucial conclusion: ***for learning to take place the reptilian brain must be satisfied that all is well - otherwise learning is biologically impossible.***

Conditions which threaten the reptilian brain:-

**Physical conditions:** hunger/thirst, too cold/hot, physical discomfort, inadequate light, overcrowding, etc.

**Emotional conditions:** anxiety/fear, lack of self esteem, sense of isolation, feeling insecure, personal worries, a sense of injustice.

In order for learning to take place, pupils' physical and emotional needs must be satisfied. The conditions which activate the reptilian brain, and close down higher order functions can be collectively termed STRESS. In order to facilitate effective learning it is essential to reduce pupils' stress.

## KEEPING THE MID BRAIN HAPPY

Where children believe that they can be capable learners they will have the high self esteem and motivation which are a pre-requisite for successful learning.

### Ways of raising self esteem:-

- Help each child to build a sense of identity as a learner
- Programme for success, not failure, for each child - set achievable goals that are just challenging enough
- Value everyone's contributions

Give unconditional positive feedback to everyone

Children need to believe that what they are learning is worth while and relevant to them personally - otherwise motivation and attention will be low.

Plan lessons according to:-

**WIIfm** - '**W**hat's **I**n **I**t **f**or **m**e?' as a pupil if I acquire this new skill, knowledge as understanding.

**CITV** - **C**onnect **I**nto **T**heir **V**alues, what will be exciting enough to compel attention, what will they consider interesting and important?

# THE LIMBIC SYSTEM

The limbic system is in the mid-brain and is the area which governs our emotions. It is the seat of our beliefs and values and our sense of identity. Through this part of the brain we attach a concept of truth to what we learn, and develop a sense of self.

Our long term memory is also situated in the limbic system - the more powerfully emotion is connected to any information, the more firmly it will be embedded in our memory, and the quicker and easier it can be recalled.

The limbic area is rich in brain chemicals - **the neurotransmitters** which help transmit messages throughout the brain. These include the endorphins - natural opiates which kill pain and make us feel good. Positive emotions help to speed up the neurons' communication process and facilitate learning.

## The Limbic System's role in learning:-

- the more emotion attached to any experience the more memorable it becomes. Children learn most effectively (and remember more) when teaching engages their emotions.
- "feeling" that something is right is the commonest way we have of "knowing what we know", or validating our learning.
- positive emotional states are crucial in learning - emotions are the driving force of learning.

The limbic system also helps to regulate attention, in conjunction with the Reticular Activating System (RAS) which is situated at the top of the reptilian brain next to the limbic system. This filters the massive amounts of data pouring in through the senses every moment and directs what is considered important to conscious attention. This is the reason for 'the cocktail party syndrome' when you hear your own name across a crowded room filled with noise. To keep children's attention, information has to have direct relevance to self.

# "IF YOU THINK YOU CAN OR YOU THINK YOU CAN'T - YOU'RE RIGHT"

Henry Ford

***"The thing always happens that you really believe in, and the belief in the thing makes it happen"*** Frank Lloyd Wright

# BELIEFS AND VALUES

Individual beliefs and values are an important aspect of learning which is not always accorded the significance it deserves.

The human brain is a multi-processor, analysing huge quantities of incoming data every minute, and working on various levels simultaneously. Some scientists suggest that the brain may in some respects be organised in a hierarchical way.

Robert Dilts' concept of neurological levels* offers a model which can be used to shed light on some of the dynamics which influence learning.

The neurological levels include:

- Self Identity (Who am I?)
- Beliefs/Values (Why do I do what I do?)
- Capabilities (How do I do what I do?)
- Performance/Behaviour (What do I do?)
- Environment (Where and When do I do it?)

As we have seen, the Reptilian Brain plays an important role in brain function and is very concerned with **ENVIRONMENTAL** issues. Teachers in many schools face considerable environmental challenges, with poor working conditions and limited resources. In order to learn, certain types of **BEHAVIOUR** are required - not just reflex actions in response to teacher-led tasks (such as filling in a worksheet) but putting learning to some active use.

**CAPABILITIES** are the link between beliefs/values and behaviour. Capabilities allow us to translate our beliefs and values into behaviour. The capability to learn is shared by all the human race.

**e.g. see Dynamic Learning* Dilts & Epstein 1995

## I ENCOURAGE THE CHILDREN IN MY CLASS TO BELIEVE IN THEMSELVES AS CAPABLE LEARNERS BY:

Our **BELIEFS AND VALUES** determine why we learn - in other words what motivates us. This level is of fundamental importance in its influence on learning. Different cultural or gender values may lead to different approaches or emphasis in learning (e.g. men don't read, it's not important to come to school on time).

Our beliefs and values stem from our sense of **IDENTITY** - who we perceive ourselves to be. Sometimes someone's sense of identity inhibits them from learning because they think that if they acquire a particular capability it will make them someone they don't want to be (e.g. a swot, a 'boff'). Sometimes we unintentionally create an identity for a child (a 'dyslexic', a problem child).

An understanding of the dynamics between the different neurological levels can be helpful in deciding what would be the most effective way of tackling a problem. If a child has trouble learning to spell, is it because they are using an ineffective strategy or because they have an unuseful (limiting) belief - e.g. spelling is really difficult, no-one in our family can spell. Or maybe they have taken on an identity - I am a bad speller.

Traditionally, teaching has tended to be focused on the capability and behaviour levels and may have not paid sufficient attention to the powerful influence belief and identity issues can have on a child's achievements.

Children need to establish strong positive identities as learners so that they feel free to take risks and fully participate in classroom activities rather than falling back on self-protection strategies. Teachers can help by tackling limiting beliefs (including their own), maintaining the highest expectations, and working to build self-esteem.

# 8 EIGHT TIPS FOR TEACHING IN THE WAY THE NEO-CORTEX LEARNS BEST

1 Help the child to understand how today's lesson connects with yesterday's or last week's.

2 Novel material or unusual artefacts will be most effective.

3 Remember WII ***fm***

4 Provide input to all the senses, build in choices and decision making, use open ended tasks - learning is not a linear process

5 Ask for concentration only in short bursts - a long session will be counterproductive.

6 Use activities which make use of unconscious learning - eg. guided visualisations, role play, using music, display relevant material just above eye level

7 Use varied material and reinforcement activities

8 The brain needs regular feedback to learn - far more than can be provided by one teacher in a class of 30+. Build in ways of providing peer or self feedback, e.g. checking answers with a calculator, peer evaluation.

## THE NEO-CORTEX

The upper part of the brain comprises 80% of the whole. It oversees higher order skills such as problem solving, development of language, pattern recognition, reflective thought, and creative expression.

The neo-cortex imposes its own sense of order on the world by the organisation of incoming data, continuing to make new connections, and expand neural pathways. Each individual has to organise their own mental maps within their brain, and create their own meaning in order to learn - meaning cannot be imposed from outside.

In building up maps and models of the world, the neo-cortex:-

- seeks out patterns and relationships
- searches for novelty
- looks for relevance for self/value in learning
- works on many levels simultaneously (multi-processing)
- works in peaks and plateaux, not on one level
- works in short spurts of concentration (attention span equals chronological age in minutes for young children, up to 35-40 minutes for adults)
- operates on a conscious and unconscious level
- needs plenty of stimulation
- accesses all senses
- requires feedback

**Everyone creates their own map or model of the world.**

# THE TWO HEMISPHERES

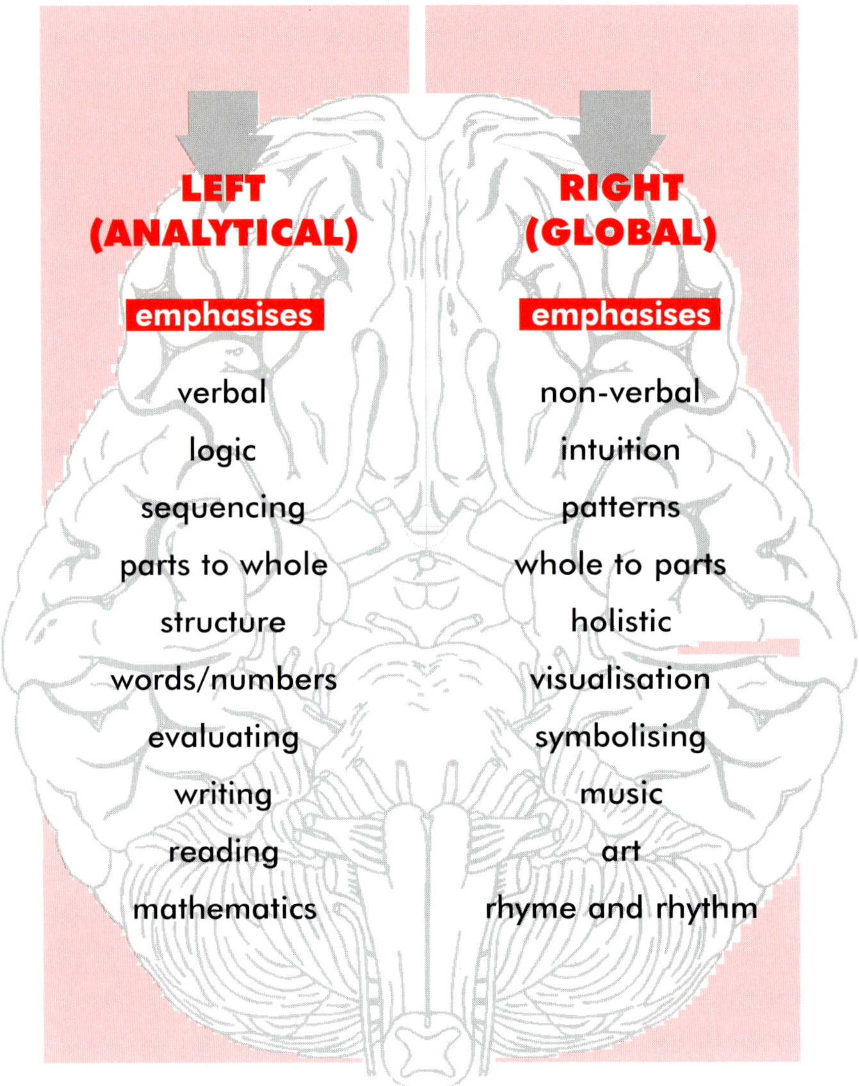

## THE HEMISPHERES

The brain is divided into two hemispheres, joined by a 'bridge' of fibres, the corpus callosum, which allows communication between the two sides. Work by Nobel prize winner Dr Roger Sperry has identified that each hemisphere specialises in different areas, and operates in different ways.

The left, or analytical, side of the brain oversees language, logic and number concepts, working in a very sequential way, from the parts to the whole. The right, or global side, is non-verbal and intuitive, dealing with visualisation, imagination, rhyme and rhythm, working from the whole to the parts.

While it is apparent that such a division of labour is by no means clear cut, this presents a useful metaphor which can move the teacher forward in facilitating learning in the classroom.

The most effective thinking and learning can take place when both sides of the brain are working in harmony together. This means offering activities which will stimulate both sides. For example, putting things to music is a useful way of encouraging learning, combining harmony (right brain) with words (left brain).

Sometime during the course of KS2, pupils may acquire hemisphere dominance for right or left brain, in much the same way as they have a dominant hand, foot, eye, and ear. Although we all use both sides of our brain all the time, hemisphere dominance can become part of our own personal learning style, and influence the way we approach learning tasks.

It is important for the teacher to recognise their own hemisphere dominance, because this may be a strong influence on how they teach. To provide the most favourable learning environment a balance of left and right brain approaches is required. The most effective learning takes place when the whole brain is stimulated and communication between the two hemispheres is flowing freely.

## ARE YOU RIGHT OR LEFT?

Try our questionnaire... page 128.

How will it influence your teaching style?

A recent discovery has highlighted an important gender difference between male and female brains. The corpus callosum has been found to be thicker - and therefore more effective - in women. The first physical evidence of women's intuition!

### Left-brain dominant learners prefer:-

- structured, sequential material and tasks
- moving from the parts to the whole
- explicit instructions
- written information
- working in a linear way, checking work

### Right-brain dominant learners prefer:-

- open ended tasks
- going from the 'big picture' to the parts
- self- selected tasks
- working from intuition, guesses, hunches

## The Big Picture

The right side of the brain likes to be given an overview of what is coming before material is presented. This is known as giving the 'big picture' or as previewing information. It enhances learning. It is useful to start the year/term/week/day/lesson by providing an outline of the learning aims for that period. Having clearly defined learning intentions, already identified as good practice for teachers, helps in this and other ways.

Previewing material 'primes' the brain, so that connections are already being made in readiness for new learning. The details can then be offered to continue the process of building new neural networks within the brain.

As will be discovered, reviewing material is also essential to effective learning. The ideal lesson plan will therefore include a preview of aims, delivery of material and a review of work covered to conclude.

# HOW THE BRAIN OPERATES

## Implications for Classroom Practice

| Implications for Teaching | What to do next |
|---|---|
| Learning takes place when neurons (brain cells) make connections with each other and neuron networks develop. | Check practice. Effective teaching builds on and expands existing knowledge, skills and understanding. Connect to previous learning. |
| The stage of myelination of a child's brain dictates developmental readiness. There is a normal age range for development of 18 months and there are gender differences. | Be aware that pupils respond differently according to their stage of brain development. |
| An enriched environment stimulates dendrite growth and new connections. | Provide stimulation in all sensory systems. |
| The brain is designed for survival, not for learning. If a child feels uncomfortable or threatened, physically or emotionally, they are biologically incapable of learning. | Take steps to ensure physical comfort and emotional security within the classroom. Boost self esteem of pupils. |
| Learning is most memorable when emotions are involved. | Add in emotional content to lessons, - humour, drama, etc. |
| Attention span is limited - think in terms of chronological age in minutes | Introduce frequent breaks and changes of direction. |
| Whole brain learning, using the strengths of both hemispheres is most effective. | Understand own hemisphere preference, and ensure that teaching methods are aimed at both L and R brain. |
| The RAS directs conscious attention to items of data which have personal importance or relevance. | Teach with CITV. Remember WIIFM. |

# ACTION PLAN

What important issues has this chapter raised for you?

What implications does this have for teaching and learning in the classroom?

What implications does this have for teaching and learning at a whole school level?

Proposed Action:

# CHAPTER TWO
# ATTENTION AND LEARNING

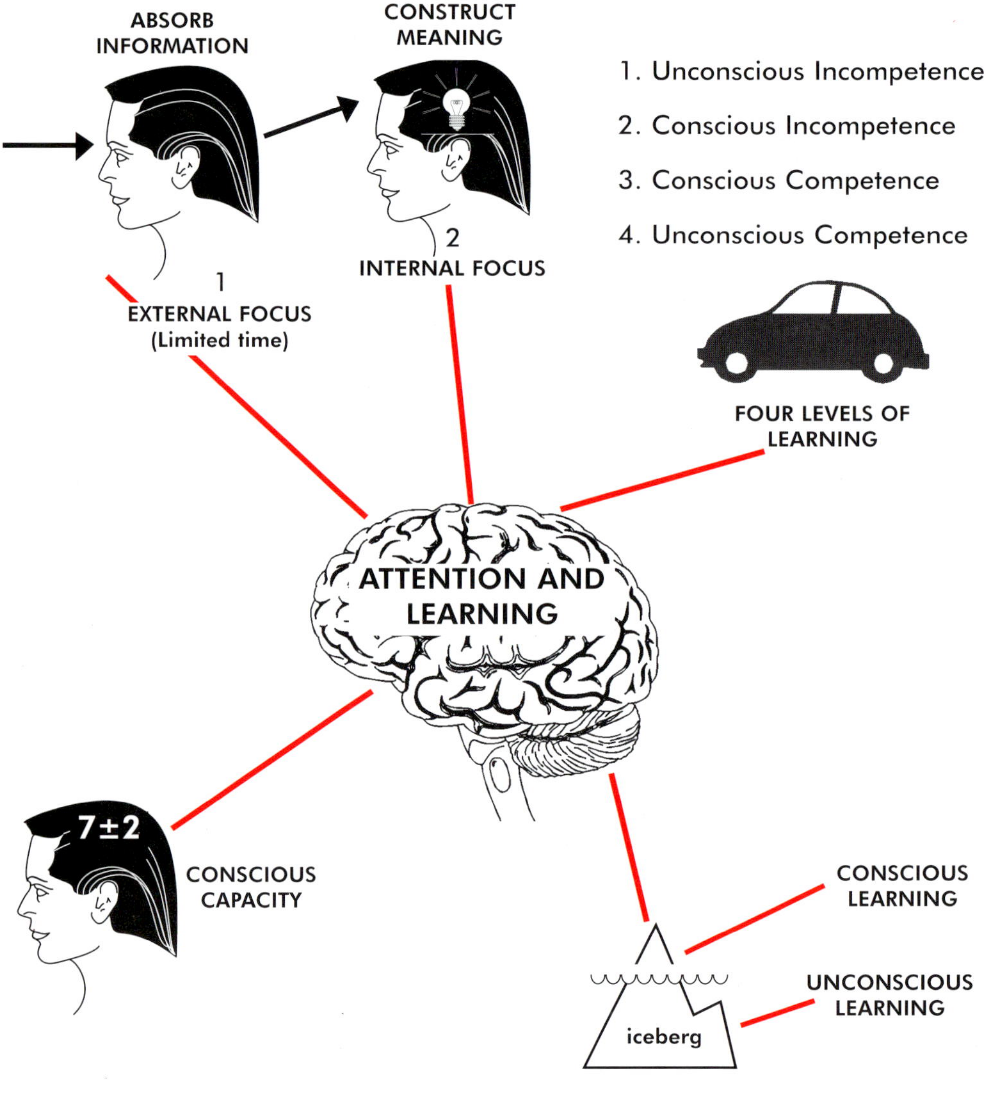


# LEARNING AND ATTENTION

Fundamental, and interrelated aspects of learning at KS 1 & 2 are:

- The absorbing of information
- The construction of meaning
- The acquisition of skills

These processes occur both inside and outside conscious awareness. Research suggests that the vast majority of learning takes place outside conscious awareness - i.e. at an unconscious level. Take the example of a child using Dienes apparatus to solve a subtraction problem with tens and units. At a conscious level the child is developing subtraction skills whilst non-consciously s/he is learning about the relationship of 1 and 10, their relative size and volume and constructing an understanding of place value.

Much of teachers' current efforts are directed towards conscious learning. It is important not to overlook techniques designed to increase unconscious learning. However let us first consider teaching and learning directed to the conscious mind.

To absorb information effectively, the conscious mind needs to be externally focused on the source of information. This may be the teacher and the board or a textbook. We can only maintain such a focus for a limited amount of time, perhaps 30 - 40 minutes for an adult, but for a child a realistic estimate would be the **chronological age (or learning age) in minutes**. This means that information should be presented to the young mind in short spurts.

Attention span will vary according to the interest of the material. High interest will be accorded to information which:

- is related to survival, including social and cultural issues
- has a high novelty value (the brain loves novelty)
- is perceived to have direct personal relevance
- has a high emotional content
- is delivered in a multi-sensory format.

## Some Exercises to See How the Brain Absorbs and Retains Information

**Excercise 1** Place a sheet of paper covering rows A to J. Move the sheet of paper down so that row A is revealed. Read out aloud the four numbers and then cover up row A and see if you can remember all four. If you are successful move onto Row B which has five numbers and then row C which has six. How far do you get before you reach the data capacity of your conscious mind?

| | |
|---|---|
| Row A | 5 1 7 9 |
| Row B | 6 3 0 5 2 |
| Row C | 1 5 3 0 4 5 |
| Row D | 5 9 6 1 0 2 3 |
| Row E | 2 1 4 2 6 3 8 4 |
| Row F | 7 9 1 6 3 8 6 1 3 |
| Row G | 1 6 3 2 4 8 6 4 8 0 |
| Row H | 6 8 9 1 6 2 0 7 9 5 9 |
| Row I | 1 3 2 6 3 9 5 2 6 5 7 8 |
| Row J | 0 9 1 8 2 7 3 6 4 5 5 4 6 |

**Excercise 2** Now try exercise two. Row A has six digits grouped together as three pairs each pair forming a number. Read out aloud the three numbers in Row A i.e. "fifteen" "thirty" and "forty five". Now cover up the row and see if you can remember the three numbers. If you can, try row B and so on.

| | |
|---|---|
| Row A | 15 30 45 |
| Row B | 21 42 63 84 |
| Row C | 16 32 48 64 80 |
| Row D | 13 26 39 52 65 78 |
| Row E | 09 18 27 36 45 54 65 |

**Excercise 3** Now study the following nine symbols for thirty seconds then cover the information up and see how many letter symbol pairings you can remember.

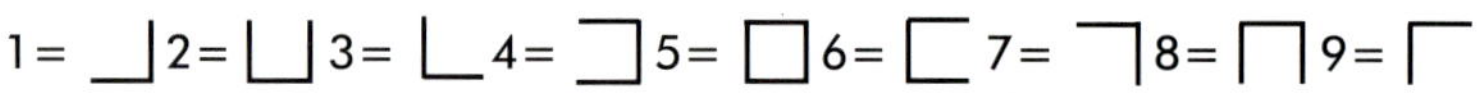


Now look at the same information presented in a different way at the bottom of page 34. Is it more easily absorbed and retained?

The number of items of information which can be absorbed in one session is also limited. George Miller proposed that 7 + or - 2 chunks of information can be held in the adult conscious mind at any one time - i.e. 5 - 9 items. Try Exercise 1 (opposite) and see how many items your mind can hold. This number will be smaller for children. Presenting a lot of information at once can therefore be simply overwhelming, and lesson plans need to concentrate on developing knowledge and understanding around a manageable amount of data.

However if the 'chunks' of information can be readily connected to what is already known, the chunk size can be increased so that more information can be consciously retained (see Exercise 2 opposite).

To construct meaning, conscious attention must be internally focused. Conscious attention cannot be internally and externally focused at the same time. It will either be externally focused to absorb information or internally focused as it processes this information to make sense of it. This means that lessons will benefit from being structured so that short "information" sessions are followed by periods when children can make this information meaningful to them by thinking about it, applying it or explaining it to others.

Both information absorption and construction of meaning take place outside conscious awareness at an unconscious level. This unconscious learning can be enhanced through appropriate material displayed on classroom walls, and the use of techniques such as teaching relaxation (which promotes 'alpha' brain waves facilitating access to the unconscious mind), using guided visualisation and music (see chapter 9). Story telling and the use of metaphors are a very effective way of teaching, allowing the brain to engage at various levels simultaneously.

At an unconscious level, the brain is absorbing information and constructing meaning all the time, from all the available data. This is the reason for what is sometimes known as the 'hidden' curriculum - the attitudes and inferences which are picked up by pupils from their surrounding environment.

## THE FOUR LEVELS OF LEARNING

### Unconscious Incompetence

I remember getting a plastic steering wheel for my fifth birthday. It stuck onto the back of the driver's seat. I spent many happy hours in the back of the car turning the wheel and going "brum brum", pretending I could drive. I was blissfully unaware of the complexities of driving or that I had yet to acquire the physical and mental skills necessary to drive a car.

### Conscious Incompetence

Shortly after my seventeenth birthday I sat behind the wheel of the family car for the first time and my father patiently explained all the controls and procedures to me. I immediately appreciated the many skills involved in driving a car and that I, as yet, had few if any of them.

### Conscious Competence

After much practice, grinding of the gears and gnashing of my father's teeth I reached a level of competence where, by concentrating hard, I could successfully drive the car for 20 minutes or so and would finish the session mentally exhausted.

### Unconscious Competence

A few years on, having passed my test and consolidated my skills through many hours of motoring, the procedures involved in driving the car were automatic. I didn't need to think about when and how to change from second to third gear. I just did it. I could think about other things as I drove. I often drove on "automatic pilot" - arriving home with no memory of the journey.

### Addendum

I recently had the enlightening experience of teaching my twin sons to drive. It required me to consciously think about how I actually drove a car and to review my practice. I quickly realised that if I took my driving test again I would certainly fail. However by consciously thinking about and reviewing my driving practice I again became a safe driver capable of passing the driving test. Moving between conscious and non-conscious competence keeps practice sharp. I guess that's true for anything we do a lot - like teaching perhaps!

Much of KS 1 & 2 is concerned with the development of key skills such as numeracy and literacy. A useful model of learning proposes 4 levels of learning:

**unconscious incompetence**
(unaware of inability to perform task)

**conscious incompetence**
(aware of inability to perform task)

**conscious competence**
(able to perform task when concentrating)

**unconscious competence**
(able to perform task automatically)

Once a skill has been acquired at a level of unconscious competence, it can be performed outside of conscious awareness, and other matters can be allowed to engage conscious attention - for example holding a conversation or listening to the radio while driving along a familiar route. Once we have achieved a level of unconscious competence, the mechanics of writing, punctuating, and even spelling, trouble us very little as we draft a report or write a lesson plan.

For a child who is still at the level of conscious competence, the task of forming letters, using capital letters and full stops and spelling words correctly, uses a significant proportion of their available chunks of conscious attention. This limits their capacity for focusing on such matters as composition, structuring their writing and using varied and stimulating vocabulary.

It is therefore helpful to be clear of the learning aims for a session. For example whilst some lessons may focus specifically on letter formation or spelling common words correctly, other sessions may concentrate more on composition skills or writing with regard for the needs of the reader. In the latter cases support can usefully be given with the mechanics of converting ideas into the written word for example the use of voice controlled word processing packages, concept keyboards or supplying spellings for key words.

# ATTENTION AND LEARNING

## Implications for Classroom Practice

| The implications for Teaching | What to do next |
|---|---|
| To learn, the brain needs to absorb information and construct meaning. | Recognise these two distinct phases of the learning process and plan for them when preparing lessons. To construct meaning, the conscious mind needs to focus internally. |
| To absorb information, the conscious mind needs to be externally focused. External attention span is approximately one minute for each year of age. | Review practice to ensure the presentation of information is in short bursts. |
| The conscious mind can only hold 7 + or - 2 items of data. | Provide a limited number of items of data in each learning session. Focus on key items. "Chunk" or connect data to maximise the amount absorbed. |
| To construct meaning, the conscious mind needs to focus internally. | Follow each "information" session with time and activities that enable pupils to construct meaning. |
| The majority of learning occurs unconsciously. | Consider the techniques you can employ to facilitate unconscious learning. |
| There are four levels of learning. Skills that can only be executed at a particular level of conscious competence use up part of available attention - limiting the concentration that can be paid to other thinking or doing tasks. | Be clear about the focus of the lesson. Is it about developing and consolidating skills and competences or is the thinking that forms part of the activity more important? |

### Exercise 3

| | | |
|---|---|---|
| 1 | 2 | 3 |
| 4 | 5 | 6 |
| 7 | 8 | 9 |

# ACTION PLAN

What important issues has this chapter raised for you?

What implications does this have for teaching and learning in the classroom?

What implications does this have for teaching and learning at a whole school level?

Proposed Action:

# CHAPTER THREE
# STATES IN LEARNING

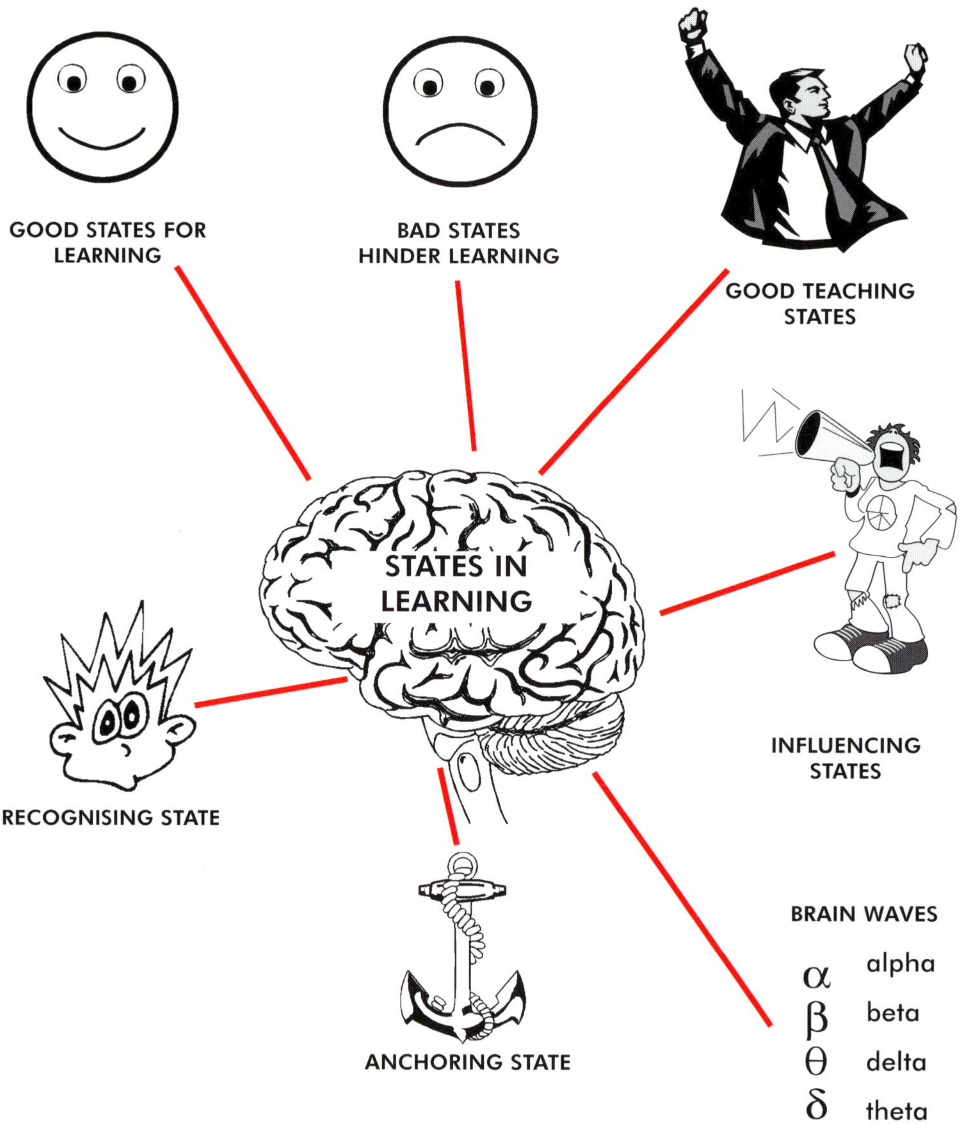

# LEARNING STATES

At any given time we are in a 'state of consciousness' - a frame of mind or mood determined by physical, mental and emotional factors.

We may describe ourselves as happy, relaxed, bored, depressed, alert, curious, impatient etc. etc. This refers to our state at that moment. Our state influences how we react to what is going on about us, including what and how much we learn.

## Learning is state dependent.

Some states are conducive to learning and some are not. Some states positively hinder learning from taking place. Trying to teach someone something if they are not in the right sort of state is like putting your foot on the accelerator when the car is not in gear - a lot of revs, but you don't go anywhere.

Our state is a product of our complex mind-body system. Physically, certain postures are linked to certain states - when did you see someone jumping up and down with depression, or drooping with excitement? We can make deductions about someone's state by minor changes in their physiology - such as posture, rate of breathing, skin colour and muscle tension. In fact, unconsciously, we do so all the time.

If we make a change in any part of the system, the whole system is affected. Simple physical activities therefore can provide a 'break state' - a way of inducing oneself or someone else to move away from an unresourceful state with a resulting change in behaviour. Certain mind/body exercises are particularly useful as break state activities.

If learning is state dependent then it seems to follow that so is teaching. Moreover, negative states can be infectious, so it is important that teachers are in a good state for teaching as well as pupils for learning.

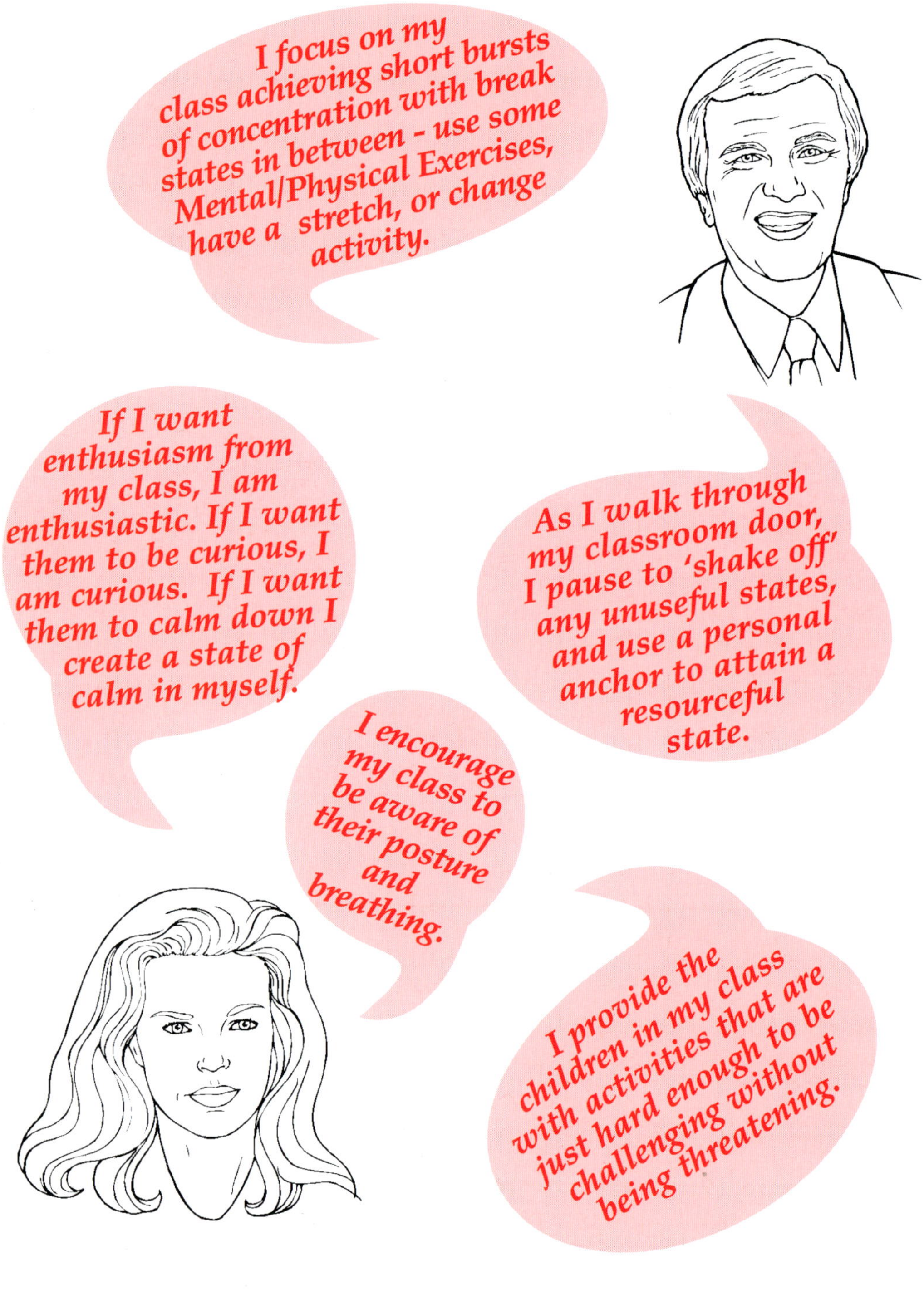
I focus on my class achieving short bursts of concentration with break states in between - use some Mental/Physical Exercises, have a stretch, or change activity.
If I want enthusiasm from my class, I am enthusiastic. If I want them to be curious, I am curious. If I want them to calm down I create a state of calm in myself.
As I walk through my classroom door, I pause to 'shake off' any unuseful states, and use a personal anchor to attain a resourceful state.
I encourage my class to be aware of their posture and breathing.
I provide the children in my class with activities that are just hard enough to be challenging without being threatening.

## STATES IN LEARNING

**Good States in Learning**

- curiosity
- interest
- anticipation
- challenge
- alertness
- motivation
- mental and physical well-being

**States which hinder or prevent learning**

- anxiety
- fear of ridicule or humiliation
- fear of punishment
- physical discomfort (hunger, cold, etc)
- boredom
- isolation

## RECOGNISING STATE

- posture (angle of head and shoulders, etc)
- gesture (e.g. use of hands)
- eye movement
- barrier signals (crossed arms, etc.)
- rate of breathing and/or pulse
- skin colour
- shape of lower lip
- facial muscle tension
- tone/pitch of voice
- tempo of speech

**What to look out for:**

Notice how your own state affects your physiology - how fast you are breathing, for example, and your tone of voice.

## BRAIN WAVES

The electrical activity within the brain as it passes messages through the neural pathways occurs in waves - similar to radio waves. Monitoring of these waves by an E.E.G machine has revealed that the brain uses four distinct frequencies –
$\alpha$ alpha, $\beta$ beta, $\theta$ theta and $\delta$ delta. Each frequency has been shown to be associated with particular thought processes. Beta waves are present during conscious logical thought, analysis, speaking and writing and are generated by much of the learning that occurs in the primary classroom. Alpha waves are associated with a more relaxed state and when combined with beta waves increase the brain's effectiveness to absorb and process information. Theta waves are characteristic of deep meditation, when flashes of inspiration may occur, while delta waves indicate deep sleep. The generation of alpha waves during the learning process can be increased through the use of relaxation techniques, visualisation and the playing of music.

# ESTABLISHING A PERSONAL ANCHOR

1. Imagine an archway standing in front of you.
2. Identify a positive state you would like to be able to return to easily. (It could be something like confidence, although it doesn't have to have a name).
3. Think of a time when you felt that way. Take yourself back to that time, so that you can see, hear and feel the way you did then. Intensify the sensations as much as possible.
4. When you have a really strong experience of how it feels to be in that positive state, step through the archway, taking the sensations with you.
5. Change position and break the state.
6. Test the anchor by stepping back through the archway and experiencing the positive state.
7. Use the anchor when required by re-entering your imaginary archway.

## ANCHORING STATES

'Anchoring'* is a term for a way of being able to access a desired state quickly and easily - either for yourself or someone else.

Have you ever been transported back in time and space by a particular smell - a perfume perhaps or the scent of wood or flowers?

Or being vividly reminded of a certain time and place when you hear an old song played on the radio? The smell or the song is the 'anchor' for the experience.

There are different ways of using anchoring to create a desired state, all useful in the classroom:-

**Spatial anchoring:** create an association over time between different places in your classroom and desired states - e.g. stand in one place to give instructions, another to give reminders about noise, somewhere else when it's time for a joke. Soon you will create an expectation about what is coming so that children automatically become alert for instructions, prepared to quieten down etc.

**Visual anchoring:** can be used to communicate with a class or an individual. This is a technique much favoured by teachers of infants, pupils will readily respond to a signal such as putting a hand in the air. A frown, a smile, a thumbs up sign - all these are examples of visual anchoring.

**Auditory anchoring:** using sound to elicit a response, something we do automatically with our tone and tempo of speech. An unusual sound will quickly gain a class's attention.

**Kinesthetic anchoring:** anchoring by touch is a particularly useful way to manage the state of individuals. A specific touch - e.g. on the shoulder, when the child is on task, sets up an anchor so that the child can then be recalled to task without the teacher having to speak.

Personal anchors can be built up with practice, allowing easy access to empowering states.

**From the developers of neuro-linguistic programming (NLP).*

## TENSION RELIEVERS

**Breathing exercises are good for relieving tension, and increasing the oxygen supply to the brain.**

1. take a long deep breath through the nose
2. hold for 2 - 3 seconds
3. exhale slowly through the mouth, relaxing the jaw and shoulder muscles and breathing away tension
4. repeat several times, throughout the day

**Practise consciously relaxing muscles which are tensed unnecessarily. Areas to watch out for include:**

- jaw
- forehead
- neck and shoulders
- stomach
- hands

Physical and mental tension are linked. Relaxing physically helps to unwind mentally.

Our posture reflects how we feel. Changing posture can change our state. To look and feel more confident, keep shoulders back and head upright.

## SMILE!

# TEACHING STATES

It is important to deal with issues of teacher stress, in order for teachers to work optimally. The same reptilian brain issues operate for teachers as for pupils, making stress management fundamentally important as a starting point for optimal teaching/learning in schools.

## Ways of approaching stress management for staff:

Ensure that there is a whole school approach by including a stress management section within the school's Health and Safety Policy which covers:

- a commitment to recognising and addressing stress issues
- ways in which staff suffering from occupational stress will be supported

## At a whole school level, stress is reduced if:

- the school has clear aims and objectives
- there is effective communication on management issues
- there is a consultative approach to management
- appraisal is used to support and enhance professional development
- jobs and responsibilities are allocated in a way that matches individual strengths and experience appropriately
- staff are supportive of each other, and there are regular opportunities for staff to meet informally
- staff feel free to raise and discuss issues which they find stressful
- staff have a sense of belonging and ownership within the school

## STATES IN LEARNING

### Implications for Classroom Practice

| The Implications for Teaching | What to do next |
| --- | --- |
| Learning is state-dependent - ie, children must be in the right state in order to be able to learn. | Recognise these two distinct phases of the learning process and plan for them when preparing lessons. |
| Teachers need to be in appropriate states to operate effectively. | Be aware of useful states for teaching in self. Notice when you are in a good teaching state. |
| It is possible to "anchor" states in order to be able to return - or help others return - to a resourceful state quickly. | Learn how to use anchors for oneself and others, and practise. |
| Up to 90% of learning takes place out of conscious awareness. Conscious attention is limited in time. | Allow time in lessons for pupils to construct their own meaning. Allow for break states. |
| The brain works on 4 main frequencies, and stimulating different frequencies contributes to effective learning. | Use different approaches to maximise learning - eg, visualisation techniques and music (See Chapter 9). |

# ACTION PLAN

What important issues has this chapter raised for you?

What implications does this have for teaching and learning in the classroom?

What implications does this have for teaching and learning at a whole school level?

Proposed Action:

# CHAPTER FOUR
# THE SENSES IN LEARNING

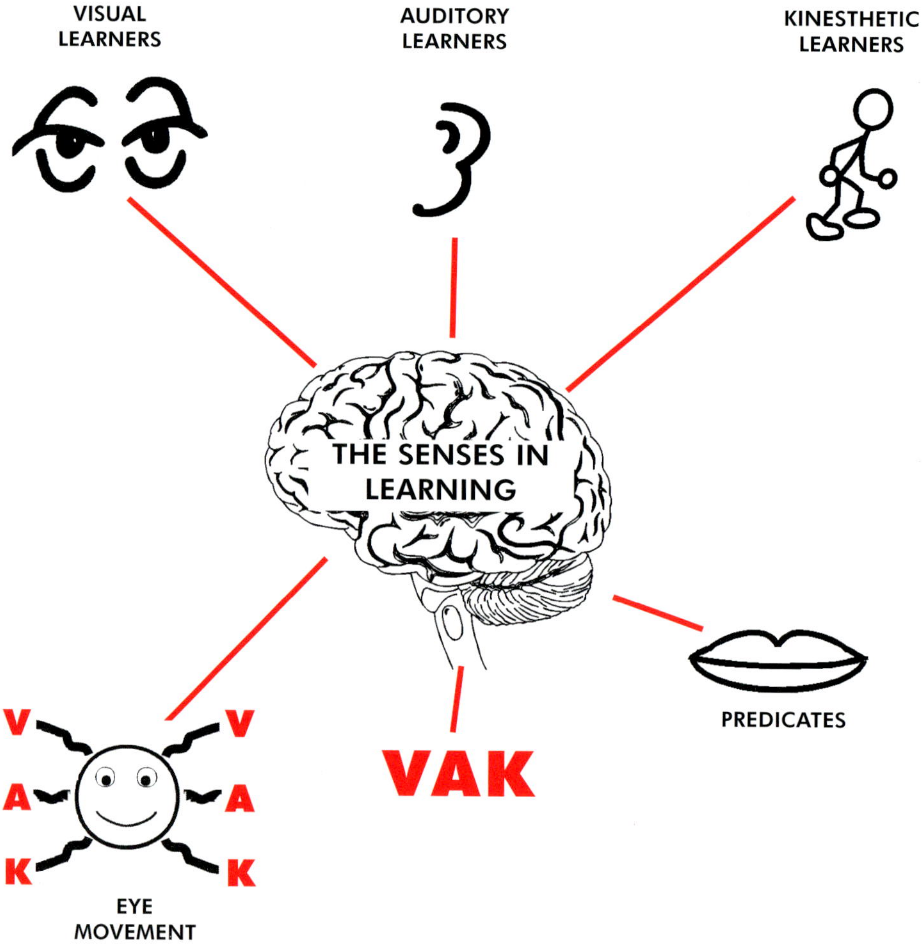

# THE SENSES IN LEARNING

We make sense of our environment by taking in vast amounts of data through our senses, and processing it to construct our own "map" of reality through our own subjective experience.

The pioneering work of Richard Bandler and John Grinder in neuro-linguistic programming (NLP) has thrown considerable light on how the human brain interprets the data received through our senses and the way in which this influences how we communicate with each other. NLP enables us to gain an understanding of our own and other people's maps of the world and the strategies we use within those maps. Understanding these processes can significantly strengthen our ability to communicate with and influence others - a skill which is at the heart of effective teaching. This makes it possible to communicate more effectively, and to facilitate the development (in ourselves and others) of the most effective strategies to approach a given task.

One of the central tenets of NLP is that the map is not the territory - all we have is our interpretation of reality, our 'map', and all maps are equally valid.

We take information about the world in through our senses, or representational systems as they are referred to in NLP.

| | | |
|---|---|---|
| **Visual** | **--** | **images** |
| **Auditory** | **--** | **sounds** |
| **Kinesthetic** | **--** | **feelings (tactile & emotional)** |
| **Olfactory** | **--** | **smell** |
| **Gustatory** | **--** | **taste** |

In practice, the olfactory and gustatory systems are often included as kinesthetic, leaving visual, auditory and kinesthetic as the main representational systems (VAK).

## Predicates - the words we use reveal the way we think

| Unspecified | Visual | Auditory | Kinesthetic |
|---|---|---|---|
| I understand | I see what you mean | I hear you loud and clear | I've got the hang of that |
| I know | That's the way it looks | So I've heard | My feelings exactly |
| That's obvious | That's clear | Tell me about it! You don't say! | That fits |
| That's confusing | I can't see it | I can't make rhyme or reason of it. | I can't take that in |
| That's my opinion | That's my point of view | It sounds to me that | That's how it strikes me |
| I understand | I can see where you're coming from | That rings a bell | I catch your drift |
| I don't understand | That's obscure | That tells me nothing | I can't grasp that |
| I don't know about that | That's over the horizon | I can't tell what will happen | That's out of my reach |
| He's insensitive | He's blind to my view | He's deaf to my words | He's unfeeling |
| Do you understand? | Do you see? | Does that sound right? | Does that feel right? |
| I want to communicate with | I want to show you | Listen carefully | I want to put you in touch with you |
| My attitude is | My perspective is | I'd say that | My stance is |

## THE SENSES IN LEARNING

Work in NLP has shown that, while we all use all of our senses all of the time, genetic inheritance and environmental experiences may result in individuals favouring one of the representational systems more than the others.

As part of the way we process data, we can recreate (remember) or imagine (construct) pictures, sounds and feelings, and we can 'talk' to ourselves through internal dialogue. Some people find it easy to do all of these, others may find one or more difficult. So while some people are quickly and easily able to summon up a mental image, some may prefer to tell themselves about their experience, and others may tend to experience the world through feelings - though we all have the capacity to use all of these.

Our preferred representational sense influences the way we learn and communicate. Our choice of language tends to reflect our sensory preference in the predicates we use, and we feel most comfortable conversing with someone who uses similar predicates.

### For example:

| | |
|---|---|
| **Visual:** | "I see what you mean"<br>"That looks like a good idea" |
| **Auditory:** | "That rings a bell"<br>"That sounds like a good idea" |
| **Kinesthetic:** | "I've got the hang of this"<br>"That feels right to me" |

The language a person uses reflects their preferred representational system. Communication is facilitated by choosing words from a person's preferred representational system when talking or writing to them. When communicating with a group ensure that all systems are represented.

# EYE MOVEMENTS

Eyes up to right - imagining a picture

Eyes up to left - remembering a picture

Eyes level and to the right - imagining a sound

Eyes level and to the left - remembering a sound

Eyes down to the right - accessing feelings

Eyes down and to the left - talking to self

Drawn as if facing person.

Note: in left handed people these eye positions may be reversed.

## THE SENSES IN LEARNING

It has been further discovered through the work of the developers of NLP, that there are certain characteristic eye movements associated with processing in different representational systems. Thus it is possible to notice from the outside the system someone is predominantly using at any one time.

### Visual:

commonly accompanied by upward eye movements. Up and to the person's left indicates they are remembering a picture. Up and to the right suggests they are constructing one. People may also have a defocused stare ahead when visualising.

### Auditory:

Level eye movements to the left or right are associated with someone remembering or constructing a sound. Looking down and to the left may show that the person is involved in 'internal dialogue' - i.e. they are talking to themselves.

### Kinesthetic:

someone with their eyes in the down right position is probably accessing their feelings.

*"I really like chocolate but when I go fishing I take worms, because that's what fish like."*

# LEARNING - IN EVERY SENSE

Whilst we receive and process information through all five senses all of the time, there may be a preference towards one system as we develop learning strategies. Teachers need to use different presentation styles and provide access to different learning materials and activities to ensure that children have opportunities to learn through their preferred representational system.

## Visually-oriented learners

respond well to:-

- the written word
- diagrams
- pictures
- videos
- wall charts and posters

## Auditorily-oriented learners

respond well to:-

- the spoken word
- lectures
- audiotapes
- discussion
- sound effects

## Kinesthetically-oriented learners

respond well to:-

- movement
- hands-on activities
- design / create activities
- role play / drama

# THE SENSES IN LEARNING
## Implications for Classroom Practice

| The Implications for Teaching | What to do next |
| --- | --- |
| Information about the world is taken in through the senses and processed to create meaning. The richer the sensory input, the more effective the learning which takes place. | Offer learning sessions which stimulate all the senses. |
| We all use all of our senses all of the time, but there may be a preferred sense which facilitates learning and shapes learning style. | Be aware that individuals differ in the ways that they learn most effectively. |
| In whole class teaching it is important that the learning styles of all children are catered for. | Review provision for visually oriented learners.<br>Review provision for auditory learners.<br>Review provision for kinesthetically oriented learners. |
| A preferred sense influences teaching style as well as learning style. | Be aware of your own preference – does this bias your teaching in any particular direction? |
| Language can be an indicator of a preference for a particular sense and this influences effective communication. | Become aware of sensory specific language in self and others.<br>Develop flexibility in use of language. |
| Eye movements can be an indicator of how an individual is processing information at a given time. | Learning to track eye movements gives clues as to how individual pupils prefer to learn. |

# ACTION PLAN

What important issues has this chapter raised for you?

What implications does this have for teaching and learning in the classroom?

What implications does this have for teaching and learning at a whole school level?

Proposed Action:

# CHAPTER FIVE
# STRATEGIES AND LEARNING STYLES

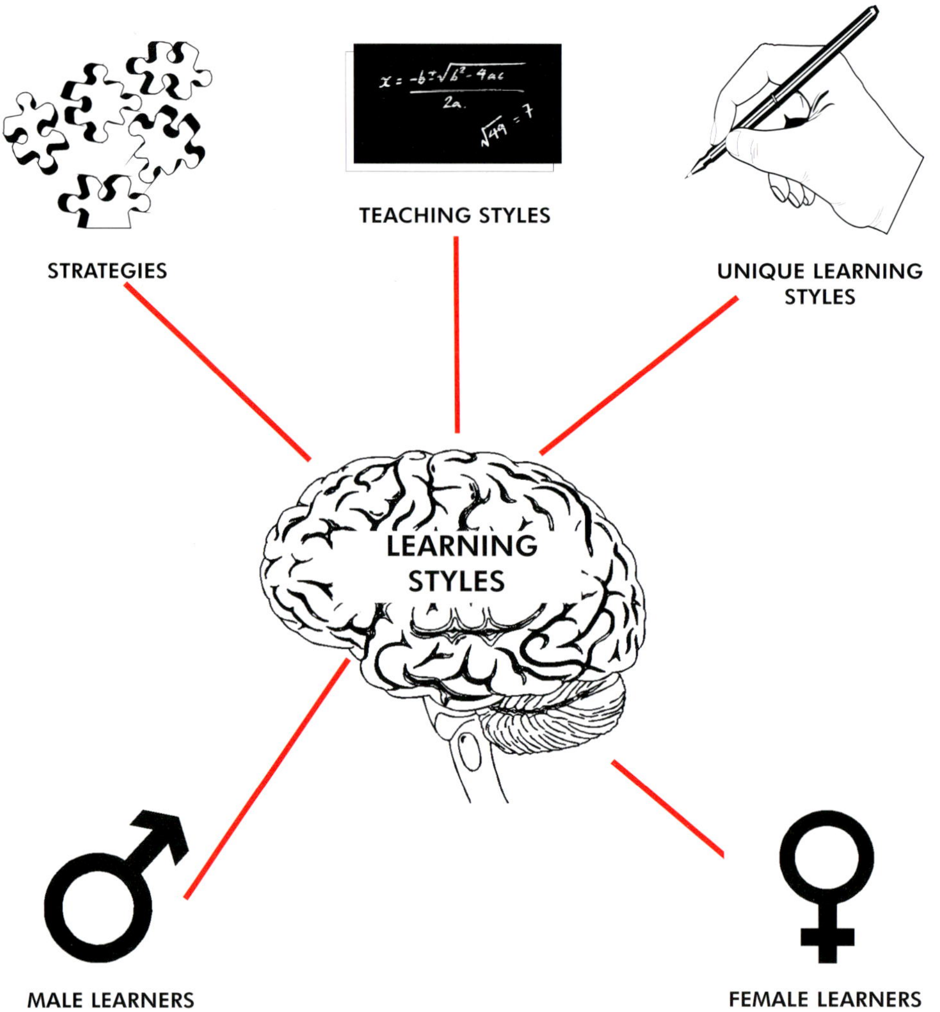

## STRATEGIES

We organise our behaviour through strategies - that is, we have a plan of action for approaching a task, whether it be choosing what to eat in a restaurant, completing a jigsaw puzzle, engaging in problem solving or learning to spell a word.

Strategies are built up through our representational systems. For example on reading a menu in a restaurant, one might see an internal image of a dish (visual), talk to oneself about it (auditory), imagine the taste (kinesthetic), and perhaps have a feeling (kinesthetic) about whether it is the right dish.

Our strategies are often developed at an unconscious level. They may be highly effective, or not so effective. In order to learn optimally, we need effective learning strategies, so it is important to teach and model useful strategies, as well as recognising when a child is using an inefficient one.

A good example is the different strategies people commonly use for learning to spell:-

The most successful spellers store and access words visually. They get a picture of a word (V), and then a feeling of familiarity (K) which tells them it is correct.

Some good spellers access words kinesthetically, because repeated writing or typing codes the spelling in motor memory.

Poor spellers are often those who access auditorily, or 'sound out' the word. This is slower and less efficient because the English language does not lend itself to phonetic construction, although it is a useful back up strategy for spelling words that have not been seen.

# "A KEY TASK FOR THE TEACHER IS TO ENABLE PUPILS TO ACQUIRE EFFECTIVE LEARNING STRATEGIES"

Many children come to school having acquired useful learning strategies from their home environment - probably at an unconscious level. Many other children do not have such strategies, either consciously or unconsciously. Raising awareness of the importance of having and choosing appropriate strategies for different learning tasks, is a crucial role for teachers, encouraging children to 'learn how to learn'. For example it is sometimes less helpful to answer a child's question than to offer ways in which they can find the answer for themself. This demonstrates that 'asking someone else' is not the only strategy and may not be the most effective one.

An example of how a teacher can explicitly teach the children an effective strategy for spelling is to use an adaptation of the NLP spelling strategy set out below.

### A modified version of the Look, Cover, Write, & Check system:-

1. Look at the word, and write it in the air with a finger, up and to the left. Letters can be vocalised internally or externally if it helps.
2. 'See' the word internally at the same time, imagining the letters in different colours. Cover the original word.
3. Read the letters from the internal image and write them down.
4. Compare the result with the internal image - does it look/ feel right? (If not, try again).
5. Check the word with the original.

(To check if a child has an internal image of a word - ask them to read the letters off backwards.)

## YOUR LEARNING STYLE IS AS UNIQUE AS YOUR SIGNATURE

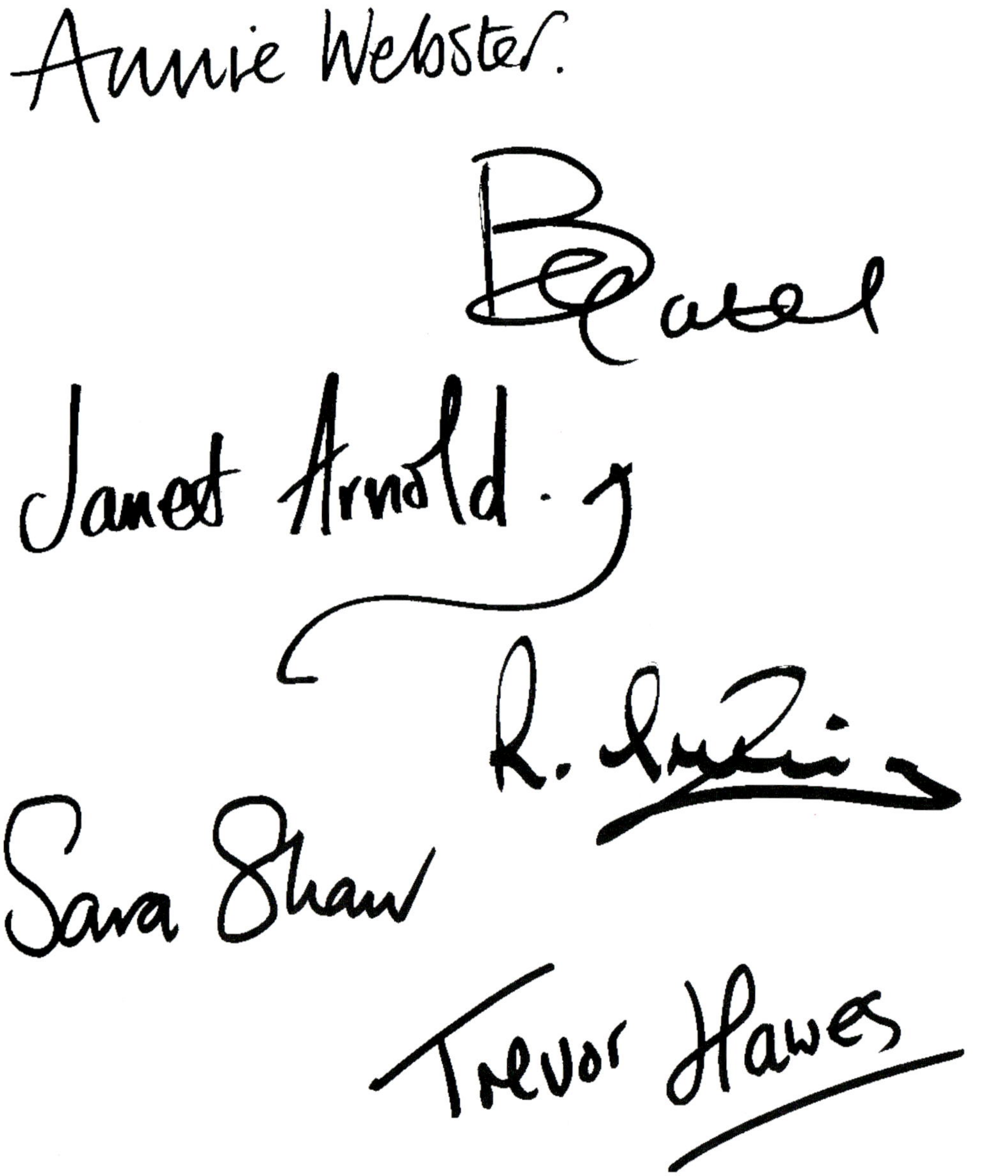

# LEARNING STYLES

Each person has a learning style as unique as their signature or their fingerprint.

Our learning style can be defined as the characteristic way in which we interact with our environment, taking in, filtering and processing data in order to enrich and enlarge our models of the world.

Learning style is made up of cognitive, biological and psychological factors such as:-

- hemisphere dominance
- representational system preference
- intelligence profile - ability to process numbers, words, music, feelings etc. (see chapter 6)
- environmental preferences - temperature, light, sound etc.
- physical preferences - best time of day, requirements for food and drink etc.
- psychological preferences - motivation, working alone or with others etc.

Learning is optimised when learning style is catered for. Teachers tend to teach in a way that suits their own learning style, so it is important to be aware of personal preferences and ensure these do not overly influence teaching practice. For example a dominantly auditory, right brained teacher might rely heavily on the spoken word and giving the big picture without a lot of structured detail. The dominantly visual, left brained teacher might write up clear and detailed numbered instructions, without first giving the big picture or allowing for open ended tasks.

In large classes, most pupils will respond to a 'scattergun' approach where their needs are being met at least some of the time. However for some children who have a strong preference, it may be necessary to pay closer attention to the requirements of their personal learning style in order to optimise their performance. Kinesthetic learners, for example, may not have their needs recognised and catered for - perhaps partly due to practical organisational difficulties.

## PREFERRED LEARNING STYLES

# LEARNING STYLES

Various models of learning styles have been offered such as those by Dunn & Dunn, and Dennison & Dennison. Dunn, Dunn & Price have published a Learning Styles Inventory:

The Learning Styles Inventory uses 5 categories to build up an individual's learning style profile - environmental, emotional, sociological, physical, and psychological.

Drawing on elements from each of these categories, the Inventory identifies the conditions under which an individual learns most readily, including the type of environment, instructional activities, social grouping and motivating factors.

## Dominance Profiles:

First developed by Dr Paul Dennison, the idea of a dominance profile refers to the lateral dominance of eyes, ears, hands, and feet in relation to hemisphere dominance.

The combination of these factors form 32 different dominance patterns which are thought to determine the ways in which individuals process information and therefore the learning experiences which will be most useful for them.

In her book 'The Dominance Factor', Carla Hannaford suggests that lateral dominance patterns have a profound effect, not only on how we learn most effectively, but on our behaviour generally, including how we interact with others.

Hannaford suggests that a mismatch between instructional methods offered in schools and the dominance profiles of some pupils has led to an increase in labelling of pupils as having learning disabilities.

## THE MALE BRAIN: 5 KEY DIFFERENCES

**Greater Compartmentalisation:** The male brain has a smaller corpus callosum - the fibres which link the left and right hemispheres. The processing of linguistic data is confined to the left hemisphere and spatial information to the right. The neural pathways tend to be stronger and more localised in the male brain. As a result the male has a tendency to use only one hemisphere and have one area of the brain active at any one time - to be focused and dogmatic.

**A larger area for Visual/Spatial Processing:** With a larger area of the brain devoted to visual/spatial processing, males tend to be better at solving three dimensional puzzles. Boys enjoy and naturally spend much of their childhood wiring up this part of the brain through construction with Lego bricks, playing football, throwing stones etc.

**A higher level of Testosterone:** The male brain contains up to 10 times more testosterone (in puberty it can be 20 times). This hormone causes humans to be more noisy, action orientated (and fidgety), competitive and aggressive. A higher level of testosterone also makes the male more concerned with his place in the pecking order, and more inclined to insult or try to score over colleagues than co-operate with them. He needs to explore the space around him and test himself.

**A lower level of Serotonin:** The brain uses this neurotransmitter to engage the logical/rational area of the brain. It enables the brain to override emotional responses produced by the mid brain area and the instinctual responses of the reptilian brain. Low levels of serotonin are associated with poor behavioural control - acting without thinking. It makes males greater risk takers. With lower levels of serotonin, boys benefit from formal teaching methods, which allow less opportunity for misbehaviour. Six out of seven pupils expelled from school are male.

**A lower level of Dopamine:** This neurotransmitter plays a central role in alerting the brain to important information and maintaining attention. The lower levels of dopamine present in the male brain mean that a greater level of stimulation is required to grab and maintain its attention. Dopamine is also responsible for the release of endorphins which produce pleasurable states and facilitate intense concentration. Boys need to experience success early on and frequently if they are to stay on task.

# GENDER AND LEARNING STYLES

Neuro-scientific research is producing compelling evidence of the important role gender plays in learning styles. By the time children arrive at primary school, differences are evident in the ways in which boys and girls approach work and play. Given the choice, boys generally prefer to spend time with other boys and engage in noisy, physical competitive games that involve them in manipulating or throwing objects. In contrast, girls generally prefer quieter and more co-operative activities, often involving role-play and verbal interaction.

In the debate over the reasons behind these behavioural differences, nurture has often been seen as the dominant factor, the explanation being sought in the different ways society responds to and treats girls and boys. However, in recent years a number of key, measurable biological differences have been discovered between the male and female brain.

For the first twelve weeks of gestation the brains of the female and male foetus are identical, but at three months the male foetus receives a high dose of androgens (male hormones like testosterone) - causing crucial changes in the developing brain. As a result the male and female brains are as distinct from each other as the male and female body. A second dose of hormones at puberty consolidates these biological differences. In addition, ongoing differences in the day to day levels of hormones and neurotransmitters (like dopamine and serotonin) present in the brain cause males and females to respond differently to the same stimuli.

The key areas where the male and female brains are biologically different and the way this affects learning and behaviour are summarised on pages 64 and 66. The extent to which an individual's brain conforms to the male/female pattern will be influenced by:

a) the level of androgens the foetal brain received (a woman receiving a relatively high level of testosterone will have some of the characteristics of a male brain whilst a the male foetus subjected to relatively low levels of testosterone may develop a brain that is female in structure).

## THE FEMALE BRAIN: 5 KEY DIFFERENCES

**Is Networked Better:** The female brain has a larger and more effective corpus callosum - the fibres which link the left and right hemispheres. This gives the female a more integrated brain and allows areas within both hemispheres to be active simultaneously when problem solving. Her reasoning produces a more rounded view - often referred to as "women's intuition". She is also able to multi-task or undertake tasks that overlap.

**A larger area for Linguistic Processing:** As a result, females learn to talk, read and write earlier than males and go on to outperform boys in English at all four Key Stages. As adults, women tend to be better at word games such as anagrams. Girls naturally enjoy wiring up this part of their brain and from an early age are more likely to talk to their toys and participate in games that involve communication.

**A lower level of Testosterone:** The absence of a high level of testosterone makes females more co-operative and less concerned with their place in the pecking order. They are far more likely to compliment rather than insult friends. Whilst boys tend to go around in gangs, girls form a limited number of close relationships with other girls based on trust and shared secrets. Girls are, in general, quieter and more compliant. They do not feel a need to explore their surrounding environment or test themselves.

**A higher level of Serotonin:** The brain uses this neurotransmitter to engage the logical/rational area of the frontal cortex and to override emotional responses produced by the mid brain area and the instinctual responses of the reptilian brain. Higher levels of serotonin in the female brain enable her to analyse data calmly and rationally. It also means she is able to control her behaviour and that she has a greater understanding of her emotions and the emotions of others.

**A higher level of Dopamine:** This neurotransmitter plays a central role in alerting the brain to important information and maintaining attention. The higher level of dopamine present in the female brain means that she is more easily aroused and needs less stimulus to sustain attention and effort. Higher levels of dopamine also explain in part why she hears better and can listen longer and more effectively - key skills in the primary classroom.

b) the level and nature of the hormones and neurotransmitters present in the brain at any point in time. For example, women perform better in visual/spatial tests when the monthly oestrogen (a feminising hormone) level is at its lowest and better in verbal/linguistic when it is at its peak.

Over the past decade schools have formulated and implemented Equal Opportunity Policies. In many cases these policies have either explicitly or implicitly espoused treating both sexes the same, using the same teaching techniques and providing identical learning opportunities. But "sameness" does not equate with equal opportunity where the learning of the two genders is concerned.

SATs results throughout the key stages show girls out-performing boys (particularly in English) and there has been much concern in recent years that boys may be falling behind girls in their education.

In their book "Why Men Don't Iron" Anne and Bill Moir argue the case that current educational practice is more suited to the learning styles generally preferred by the female brain, with an emphasis on reading and writing skills combined with tasks that are co-operative and non-competitive, sedentary and requiring sustained attention or effort. The Moirs have referred to this as a process of "feminisation" of the classroom.

If the male brain is to learn effectively it needs loud dramatic lessons, with short information sessions followed by tasks that involve action, touching and doing, and activities which have an element of competition and challenge.

A number of primary schools are tackling this issue by dividing the boys and girls up for part of the curriculum (e.g. Year six maths) to enable different learning styles to be employed. Others are using boy/girl pairings to complement each other's strengths and weaknesses.

# STRATEGIES AND LEARNING STYLES

## Implications for Classroom Practice

| The Implications for Teaching | What to do next |
|---|---|
| We organise our behaviour, including learning, through strategies. Some strategies are very effective for the purpose, and some are less so. | Bring strategies into conscious awareness. Look for them in self and others. |
| Some children arrive at school with effective learning strategies already in place. Others do not. | Make the teaching of learning strategies explicit. Encourage children to identify and share their strategies. |
| Each individual has a unique learning style, and can learn most effectively that way. | Build up a picture of each child's preferences in terms of how they like to learn. |
| Some children have a very strong need to learn in a particular way – e.g. highly kinesthetic children, and may find it difficult to learn in other ways. | Identify children with a very dominant learning style, and aim to provide extra opportunities for them to learn in that way. |
| Our learning style influences our teaching style, so it may be easier to teach pupils with a similar learning style to our own. | Be aware of your own learning style (L/R brain, VAK, etc.) and how this might affect your teaching. |
| The male and female brains are biologically different. They have different attitudes, aptitudes and learning styles. | Consider the teaching practices which enable each gender to learn most effectively and provide appropriate learning opportunities. |

# ACTION PLAN

What important issues has this chapter raised for you?

What implications does this have for teaching and learning in the classroom?

What implications does this have for teaching and learning at a whole school level?

Proposed Action:

# CHAPTER SIX
# UNDERSTANDING AND DEVELOPING INTELLIGENCE

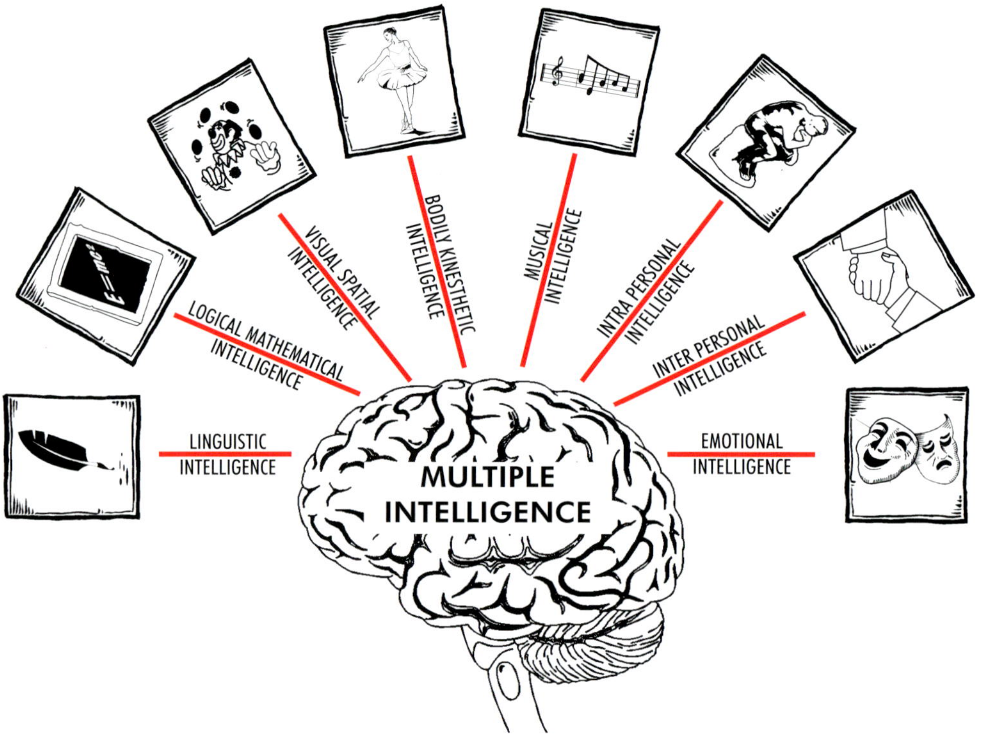


## WHAT IS INTELLIGENCE?

The definition "the ability to operate successfully in your environment" suggests intelligence can take many forms.

# INTELLIGENCE

## What is intelligence?

Over the 20th Century there has been a widespread view that our ability to learn depends on how 'intelligent' we are, and that this can be measured using paper and pencil tests which reveal our 'IQ'.

'IQ' has been thought to be a fixed limit on an individual's capacity to learn - which leads to children being regarded as more or less able than their peers.

Dr. Howard Gardner of Harvard University has developed a theory of Multiple Intelligence, comprising at least seven different types of intelligence which are not fixed but are capable of development and expansion.

Gardner's research on what constitutes intelligence demonstrates that:

- IQ tests measure only a small part of what might be regarded as constituting 'intelligence'
- genetic and environmental factors result in each of us having a different endowment of each intelligence
- the rate at which each individual develops their intelligences varies
- there is no limit (except life span!) to how far intelligence can be developed

Gardner suggests that cultural considerations influence what is valued as intelligence. The development of the IQ test in the early 20thC reflected and perpetuated the high status accorded to linguistic and logical-mathematical skills. Now it is time to consider the all round potential of each individual.

Gardner regards intelligence as: 'the ability to solve problems or fashion products that are of consequence in a particular cultural setting or community'.

He argues for education which values all the different aspects of intelligence, not just those which can be easily measured using paper and pencil tests.

## THE QUESTION ISN'T

# HOW INTELLIGENT IS THE CHILD?

## BUT

# IN WHAT WAYS IS THE CHILD INTELLIGENT?

# GARDNER'S 7 INTELLIGENCES

Gardner has identified seven areas of intelligence, present in each individual to a greater or lesser extent and capable of further development.

Linguistic intelligence: relating to language and expression through words written or spoken.

Logical-mathematical intelligence: relating to mathematical and scientific approaches, manipulation of numbers and abstract symbols, logical structured approach to problem solving.

Visual-spatial intelligence: relating to visualisation and manipulation of images, construction of models, understanding of spatial relationships.

Bodily-kinesthetic intelligence: relating to movement and use of the body in controlled ways.

Musical intelligence: relating to a sensitivity to music, sound and rhythm.

Interpersonal intelligence: relating to a sensitivity towards other people, understanding and predicting their responses, and communicating well.

Intrapersonal intelligence: relating to a sense of self and awareness of own feelings, strengths and weaknesses.

Teaching through the 7 intelligences expands the opportunities for all pupils to construct their own meaning in the way most appropriate for them. It also enables children to demonstrate their knowledge in the most effective way for them, thus showing more clearly what a pupil is capable of and raising their self-esteem in the process.

Estimates suggest that 70% of the National curriculum is geared towards just two intelligences – linguistic and logical-mathematical, thus limiting the learning experience children receive. Use of all 7 intelligences helps children to develop the skills they need to interact successfully with their environment.

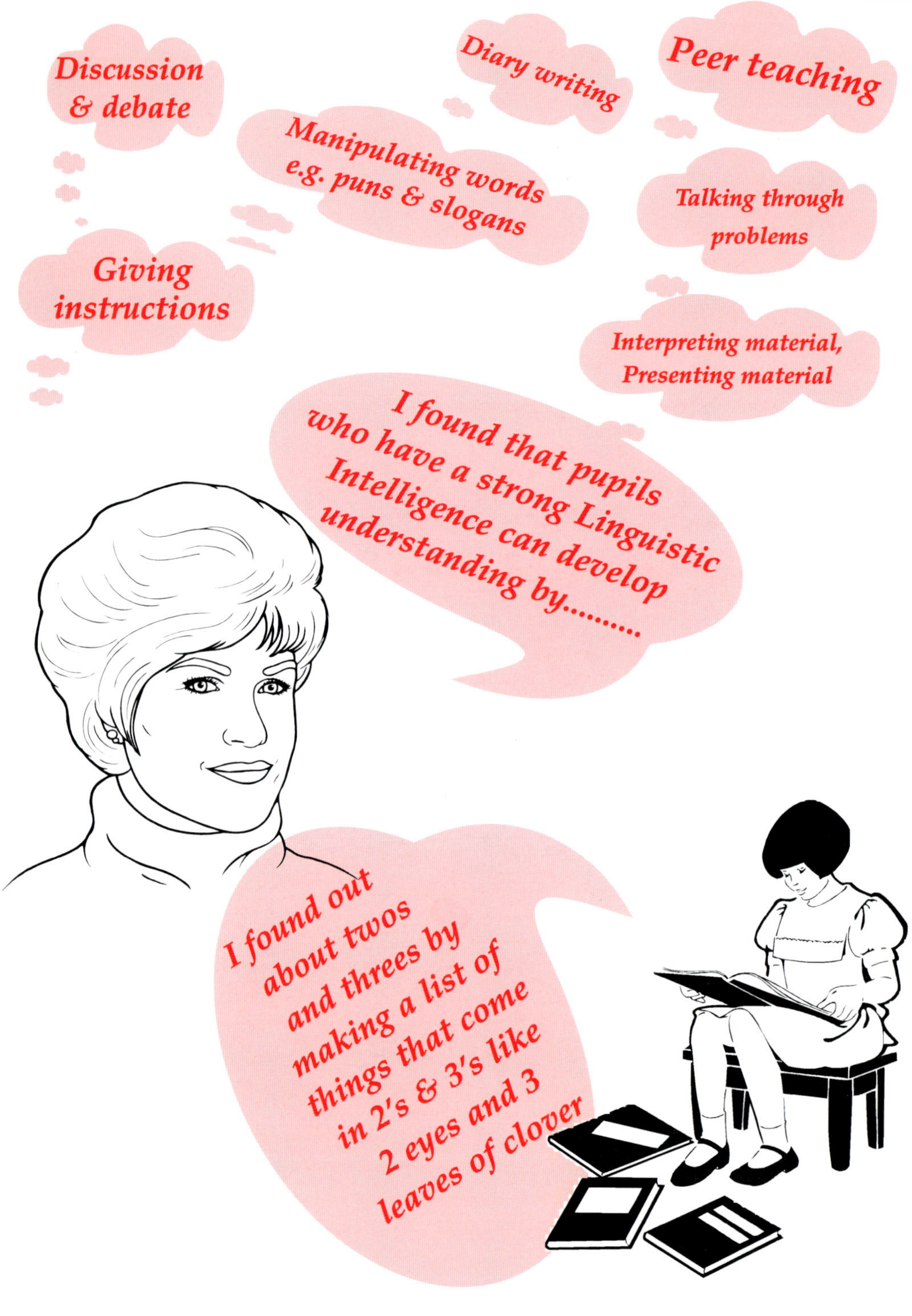
Discussion & debate
Diary writing
Peer teaching
Manipulating words e.g. puns & slogans
Talking through problems
Giving instructions
Interpreting material, Presenting material
I found that pupils who have a strong Linguistic Intelligence can develop understanding by.........
I found out about twos and threes by making a list of things that come in 2's & 3's like 2 eyes and 3 leaves of clover

# LINGUISTIC INTELLIGENCE

The Linguistic Intelligence is exemplified by those who have a good command of language, both written and spoken. They have a large vocabulary and enjoy reading, writing and speaking.

## Linguistic Intelligence:-

### Characteristics:

- good with language and manipulation of words,
- aware of patterns
- a sense of order and ability to reason
- reads, writes and spells easily
- good memory for detail

### Found in:

- poets, writers, journalists, broadcasters, politicians, teachers etc.

### Activities which strengthen:

- brainstorming, debates, discussion, speaking to an audience
- writing letters, stories, diaries, poetry, instructions, lists, book reviews, reading, retelling stories, identifying with characters, extracting information from text, using library
- building vocabulary through word games and puzzles, writing tongue twisters
- telling jokes and riddles

Comparing & contrasting ideas
Challenges
Problem Solving
Pupils who are strong in the logical mathematical intelligence respond well to..........
Making & solving puzzles
Analysing material
Managing projects
I found out about twos and threes by working out all the numbers I could divide by both two and three...like 6 and 12

# LOGICAL MATHEMATICAL INTELLIGENCE

Logical Mathematical Intelligence is seen in those who have the ability to recognise logical and numerical patterns. They enjoy solving mathematical problems in daily life, classifying and analysing information, using reasoning and making predictions.

## Logical Mathematical Intelligence:-

### Characteristics:

- good at manipulating numbers
- picks out patterns and relationships
- deals in abstract symbols
- enjoys problem solving and applying logic
- values precision and order

### Found in:

- mathematicians, scientists, engineers, accountants, economists, doctors etc.

### Strengthening Activities:

- encourage awareness of number in the environment
- following directions to accomplish a goal
- teach problem-solving strategies
- classification, sorting, Venn diagrams
- sequencing, use of symbols
- pattern identification, code making/breaking
- hypothesising, predicting, experimenting
- logic and reasoning puzzles

If a child is good Visually & Spatially I find they get on well with tasks that involve....
Map reading Map-making
Designing posters/logos
Wall displays including pictures, charts & diagrams
Building activities
Using imagination, Guided imagery
Concept maps
I made a Venn Diagram that showed numbers that could be divided by 2, numbers that could be divided by 3 and numbers that could be divided by 2 & 3

# VISUAL SPATIAL INTELLIGENCE

People with a high degree of Visual Spatial Intelligence have the ability to understand the position of self/other person/object in relation to other people or objects.

They can visualise objects in 3D, and manipulate their internal images.

## Visual Spatial Intelligence:-

### Characteristics:

- good at visualising images in 3D
- can rotate and manipulate mental images
- facility with maps, charts and diagrams
- may think in pictures
- can predict the effects of movement (self or object)
- able to design/construct 3D objects

### Found in:

- architects, navigators, engineers, artists, sculptors, chess players etc.

### Strengthening activities:

- construction/art/sculpture
- guided visualisations
- tessellation, patterns
- making maps, charts, graphs, diagrams
- concept-mapping
- illustrating or interpreting through pictures
- using imagination and fantasy
- design

Role play
Sports
Cross-lateral exercises
Dramas, Dance
I let my kinesthetic learners construct meaning through……
Field trips
Construction activities
Material they can manipulate
I found out about twos and threes by using bricks to build 2 tower blocks.
One tower block had every second floor red, the other had every third floor red. Some floors like 6 & 12 were red in both towers

# BODILY KINESTHETIC INTELLIGENCE

Bodily Kinesthetic Intelligence is typified by those who have a high degree of control over body movements, and manipulate objects easily. Children high in this intelligence do not like to sit still for too long.

## Bodily Kinesthetic Intelligence:-

### Characteristics:

- very good control of body eg. in sports or dance
- enjoys physical movement
- well-developed sense of touch
- likes to manipulate objects
- likes to participate
- may fidget and find it difficult to sit still

### Found in:

- athletes, gymnasts, dancers, surgeons, crafts people, actors etc.

### Strengthening activities:

- drama, mime and role play
- all forms of PE and dance
- human sculptures, graphs and tableaux
- field trips
- hands-on learning, construction and manipulative activities
- incorporate movement into lessons
- 'Simon Says' type games and action rhymes

Dance

Singing

Making sound effects to describe something

Listening

Children can use their musical intelligence to learn by.........

Composing rhymes & jingles

Use of instruments

Putting material to raps and tunes

Some of us used metronomes and 2 and 3 beat bars to learn about twos and threes

# MUSICAL INTELLIGENCE

Those with high levels of Musical Intelligence show the ability to translate sounds from the environment into patterns and rhythm. They are able to clap in time, sing, dance etc.

## Musical Intelligence:-

### Characteristics:

- highly developed musical intelligence may be apparent at a very young age
- sensitive to pitch, tone and rhythm
- enjoys listening to music, aware of different instruments
- facility with playing one or more instrument(s)
- good sound discrimination

### Found in:

- musicians, conductors, composers, piano tuners, recording technicians etc.

### Strengthening activities:

- use raps and chants to aid memory
- make/play musical instruments
- singing, chanting, choral reading
- use music to set moods and enhance learning
- rhythm activities including patterns
- compose and perform tunes and songs
- encourage awareness of sounds in the environment

Pupils who are strong in the interpersonal intelligence respond well to.........
Group work, Role play
Co-operative learning e.g. joint projects
Peer coaching
Activities which include communication
Peer assessment
Activities involving empathy
The teacher let a group of us make a game with 2 dice that had only twos and threes

# INTERPERSONAL INTELLIGENCE

Interpersonal Intelligence is shown in the ability to influence other people, to anticipate their likely reactions and empathise. Those strong in this intelligence are good at conflict resolution, negotiation and persuasion, and work well in teams.

## Interpersonal Intelligence:-

### Characteristics:

- good understanding of people, ability to mix easily
- sensitive to moods and intentions
- works well in a team
- communicates well with others
- empathises, able to predict peoples' reactions
- enjoys company, sociable

### Found in:

- counsellors, sales people, managers, personnel workers, teachers, politicians, religious leaders etc.

### Strengthening activities:

- collaborative work in groups
- peer tutoring, working in pairs
- team games
- role-playing
- circle time and self esteem activities
- giving and receiving feedback and constructive criticism
- group discussions and projects
- teach strategies for dealing with conflict

Self managing tasks
Goal setting
Self assessment
Self discipline
I make sure my pupils who enjoy using their intrapersonal intelligence have an opportunity for....
Guided visualisations
Reflection of personal learning style
Activities which invlove 'put yourself in this position' or 'how would you feel if...'
I made a list of all two and threes in my world. Like I have 2 gold fish and 3 trees in my garden

# INTRAPERSONAL

Intrapersonal Intelligence is seen in the capacity for reflection and self-evaluation, and the ability to think about thinking. People with high levels of this intelligence work well alone and ask penetrating and philosophical questions.

## Intrapersonal Intelligence:-

### Characteristics:

- well-developed self-knowledge
- strong sense of values
- aware of own strengths and weaknesses
- self-motivated
- well-developed sense of identity

### Found in:

- philosophers, theologians, counsellors, novelists, psychiatrists, psychologists etc.

### Strengthening activities:

- autobiographical writing and journals
- personal goal setting
- circle time and self esteem activities
- discussions about feelings and moods
- teach study skills
- provide opportunities to make and explain reasoned choices
- self evaluation

# MULTIPLE INTELLIGENCE OBSERVATION SHEET

## (a sheet for teachers to record pupil's strengths)

**Name:**

Tick as appropriate ✓ ✓

| LINGUISTIC | ✓ | LOGICAL-MATHEMATICAL | ✓ |
|---|---|---|---|
| Enjoys words (reading, writing, speaking) | | Recognises and understands patterns easily | |
| Will speak publicly | | Recognises and uses sequences | |
| Selects appropriate vocabulary | | Enjoys puzzles | |
| Can use words to present a point of view persuasively | | Uses good reasoning skills for age | |
| | | Uses strategies or formuale to solve problems | |
| **VISUAL SPATIAL** | | **BODILY-KINESTHETIC** | |
| Likes to draw and doodle | | Likes to move around | |
| Manipulates a variety of media competetently | | Has good co-ordination | |
| Can follow directions to make a model | | Likes to express self through gesture and movement | |
| | | Enjoys P.E. and exercise | |
| | | Skilled in sports and games | |
| **MUSICAL** | | **INTERPERSONAL** | |
| Enjoys listening to music | | Makes friends easily | |
| Sings, hums or whistles during the day | | Works well in a group or team | |
| Enjoys rhythm - may tap feet or fingers | | Perceptive of other people's feelings | |
| Enjoys making up rhymes and songs | | Organises others effectively | |
| **INTRAPERSONAL** | | **INTRAPERSONAL** | |
| Identifies own feelings and emotions | | Works well alone | |
| Knows own strengths and weaknesses | | Self-motivated | |

# EMOTIONAL INTELLIGENCE

Gardner recognises emotional issues within his two personal intelligences (Interpersonal and Intrapersonal). In his book 'Emotional Intelligence', Daniel Goleman addresses this subject in detail. He maintains that emotional and social skills area crucial aspect of learning, and uses the term 'Emotional Literacy' to describe skills in handling emotions and getting along with other people. He argues that the development of children's Emotional Intelligence should form a crucial part of the school curriculum.

## Emotional 'literacy' includes:-

- recognising feelings and naming them
- recognising the link between thoughts, feelings and reactions
- recognising and respecting differences in how people think about things
- being able to manage emotions ie. what triggers them, how to handle them, monitoring self talk
- self awareness, recognising own strengths and weaknesses
- possessing empathy, understanding others' feelings and how to take their perspective
- judging the consequences of alternative choices
- taking responsibility for decisions and actions
- learning to listen and ask questions appropriately
- learning the difference between assertiveness and aggression
- understanding group dynamics, co-operating, understanding when to lead and when to follow
- learning skills such as co-operation, conflict resolution, negotiation and compromise
- distinguishing between what someone else says and does, and one's own reactions and judgments.

# UNDERSTANDING & DEVELOPING INTELLIGENCE

## Implications for Classroom Practice

| The Implications for Teaching | What to do next |
| --- | --- |
| Intelligence can be expressed in a number of different ways. | Review practice – do you allow scope for the children to use all their intelligences? |
| There is no fixed limit on intelligence. | Make sure your pupils know that we all have the capacity to continually expand our intelligences. |
| We should recognise and value all intelligences as well as those which we are required to formally assess. | Review practice – in assessing children do you rely heavily on paper and pencil tests, or do you recognise achievements which are expressed differently? |
| Each individual has their own intelligence profile, and may find it easier to access curriculum material through a particular intelligence (e.g. painting a poster or making a model rather than writing prose). | Discover your own intelligence profile (see appendix). Is your teaching biased towards your own strengths? |
| Emotional intelligence underpins learning in the classroom. | Continue to teach 'emotional literacy' and model it in the classroom. |
| Using one intelligence may help to expand and develop others – e.g. the research which shows that teaching pre-schoolers to play the piano improves their mathematical and problem solving skills. | Design activities which draw on different intelligences. |

# ACTION PLAN

What important issues has this chapter raised for you?

What implications does this have for teaching and learning in the classroom?

What implications does this have for teaching and learning at a whole school level?

Proposed Action:

# CHAPTER SEVEN
# MEMORY - EFFECTIVE RETENTION AND RECALL

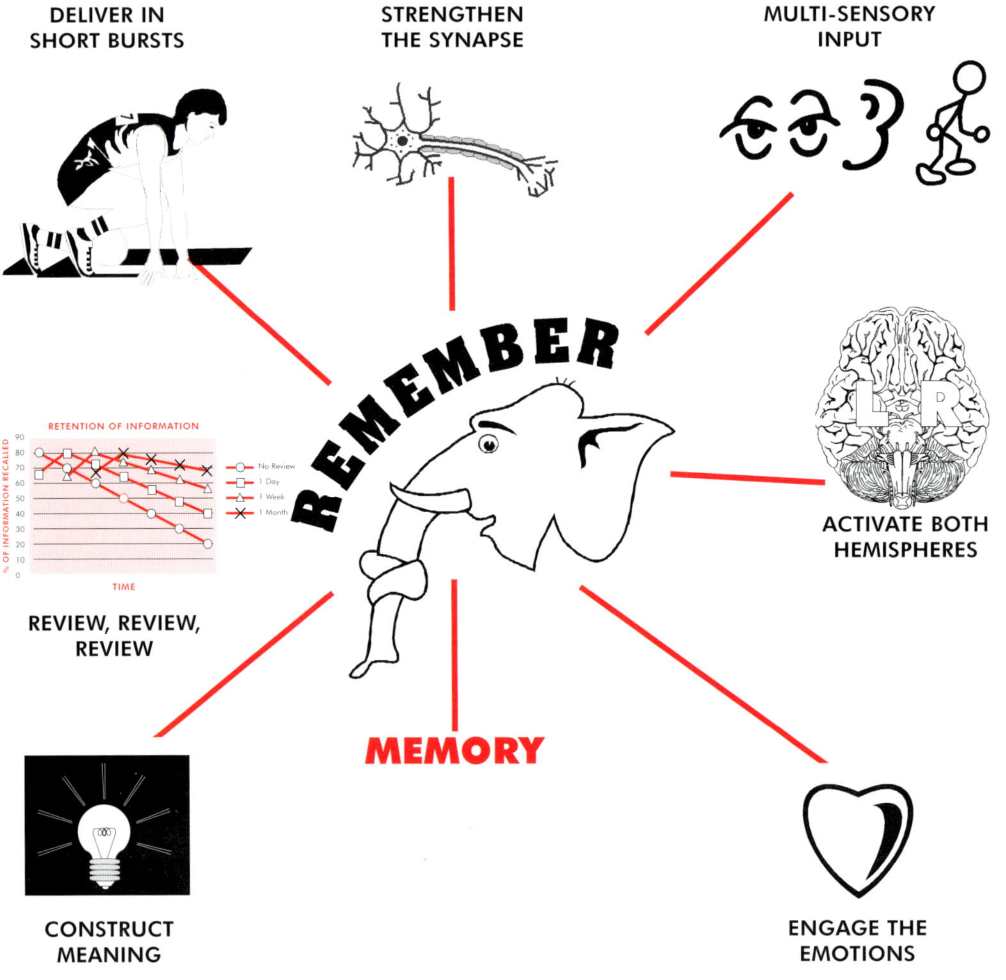

# MEMORY IS ESSENTIAL TO THE LEARNING PROCESS

Effective learning is characterised by the child's continuing ability to remember and use the skills and knowledge she/he has been taught. In other words, skills and knowledge must be stored in the long term memory and be capable of being recalled.

The introduction of the National Curriculum put a great deal of emphasis on the content of what children must be taught. The effort of fitting everything in to the school year has been likened to taking the children on a high speed train journey from London to York, and then asking them to describe the scenery. In order that children retain and are able to recall what they have learned, it is important to teach in a way that is compatible with the human memory.

## The Human Memory

The human memory system is complex and not fully understood.

Neuroscientific research has established that the human brain has:

- a short term memory that can hold 5 to 9 items of data, (on average 7 items)
- and a variety of longer term memory systems operating in various parts of the brain which combine to memorise and recall a particular fact, object, feeling, skill or experience.

Short term memory is the brain's working memory. It can hold information for up to 15 seconds – long enough to read and make sense of all the words in a sentence or mentally multiply 7 by 45. On completion of the task the short term memory is emptied. Important information gathered or generated in the short term memory may be passed in to long term memory for future use.

## The Brain's Long Term Memory Systems Include:

**EPISODIC MEMORY:** Our ability to recall events, what happened in what order, lies in our episodic memory. It is a powerful memory system. Information embedded in a story is usually recalled well. It is a memory system that human beings used for millions of years to communicate information before the advent of the printed word.

**SEMANTIC MEMORY:** Allows the brain to attaching meaning to words. Our knowledge of what an apple is, or who is the queen of England is held in semantic memory.

**MOTOR MEMORY:** The information required to ride a bike, swim breast stroke and form letters are all held in the motor memory. A powerful memory system – you never forget how to ride a bike, even if you haven't done so for years.

**CONTEXTUAL MEMORY:** Being able to recall where you were when a particular event occurred (e.g. the death of Princess Diana) is dealt with by the contextual memory. Information is often more memorable if it is acquired in a particularly relevant or unusual setting e.g. a field trip.

**VISUAL MEMORY:** Remembering and recognising images is dealt with by visual memory. It is usually characterised by eye movement upward and to the left and may be a strong memory system for visual learners.

**AUDITORY MEMORY:** Remembering and recognising sounds is dealt with by auditory memory. It is usually characterised by eye movement sideways and to the left and may be a strong memory system for auditory learners.

**KINESTHETIC MEMORY:** Remembering and recognising feelings and sensations is dealt with by kinsethetic memory. It is usually characterised by eye movement downward and to the right and may be a strong memory system for kinesthetic learners.

**Long Term Memory:** Neuroscientists have defined lasting memory as the Long Term Potentiation (LTP) of the synapse.

In chapter one we explained that, at a biological level, the brain functions by passing messages between its neurons or brain cells by a combination of electrical and chemical processes. Electrical impulses send the message down the axon, while neurotransmitters (brain chemicals) enable the message to pass across the synapse and stimulate the dendrites of the receiving neuron. Thus neurotransmitters act as a kind of ferry, carrying messages across the synaptic gap between neurons. The brain has a number of different chemicals it can use as neurotransmitters. It can also vary the strength of the chemical and thereby the strength of the message. Different combinations of electrical and chemical transmissions form a highly sophisticated messaging system.

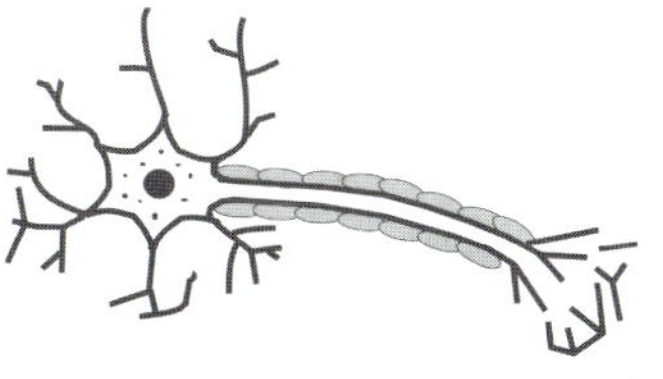

Long term potentiation of the synapse occurs when one neuron has established a relationship with another so that the stimulation of the first neuron automatically results in a message being passed to the second and subsequent neurons in a pathway – like a domino rally when the first domino topples.

Neuroscientists believe that increased potentiation is achieved in some combination of the following ways:

- myelination – which coats the transmitting axon in an insulating sheath thereby enabling the electricity to flow more efficiently
- training the neurotransmitters – the efficiency of the chemical transmission of information is increased by repeated use
- the strength of the neurotransmitter – strong emotions such as fear can form a learning pathway very quickly.

## 10 TIPS FOR MEMORABLE TEACHING

A brain is able to retain and recall information that:

1. Is presented in short bursts. We remember far more of the information from the start and finish of presentations and tend to forget the bits in between. Try to break up the day in to mini-sessions, thereby maximising the number of starts and finishes.

2. Is regularly reviewed. Research shows that up to 80% of information may be forgotten if it is not reviewed. Teachers should plan to review key facts at least five times during the lesson and briefly the following day, week and month. Use questions and quizzes to review material.

3. Engages the emotions. The strength of the neural connections made when the emotions are aroused is significantly greater. It is as if the brain puts down a marker to say this experience (e.g. touching a hot kettle for the first time) is worth remembering. The emotional content of lessons can be increased through the use of humour, creating anticipation.

4. Is used to construct meaning. Making information mean something to oneself increases both the strength and number of neural connections – thereby aiding recall. For example a child is far more likely to remember what they have learnt about electricity if they are given the opportunity to make and break a circuit. A very effective way to facilitate the construction of meaning is to get a child to explain to someone else what they have learnt.

5. Is multi-sensory thereby utilising several memory systems. It has been suggested that we remember 20% of what we read, 30% of what hear, 40% of what we see, 50% of what we say, 60% of what we do and 90% of what we read, hear, see, say and do!

## 10 TIPS FOR MEMORABLE TEACHING

6. Is presented in context. When information is presented in a supporting context the brain makes more associations and constructs more meaning. This makes data more memorable . Children will recall field trips when other lessons have been long forgotten.

7. Engages both hemispheres. That we find it easier to remember the lyrics to songs than the words to poems is due to the fact singing stimulates both hemispheres (words/left brain and music/right brain. Whole brain activities include drawing concept maps, using rhyme and rhythm when reciting facts (e.g. times table) or playing baroque music in the background when reviewing data (see page 111).

8. Is relevant or important to the individual. The brain is selective about the information it transfers to long term memory. Items of data that are important or relevant to a child are far more likely to be remembered. Identify and explain why it is important to remember the key facts and make them relevant to the child.

9. Connects to prior knowledge. The more associations or connections we can make between a new item of data and things we already know the easier it is to recall. E.g. clouds are made up of water vapour – like steam from the kettle. Topic work is particularly useful in enabling associations or connections to be made.

10. Employs memory strategies. We remember the five features of good targets through associating it with the word "SMART" (Specific, Measurable, Achievable, Reviewed & Timetabled). If you needed to remember the PIN number for your cash withdrawal card was 5487, using the phrase "Money From Electric Machine" (which has 5 letters, 4 letters, 8 letters 7 letters) makes the numbers much more memorable. Use memory strategies or mnemonics to ensure information is retained and recalled.

## REVIEWING FOR EFFECTIVE RETENTION AND RECALL.

Up to 80 percent of information will be lost if not reviewed. Information should be reviewed five times during the first learning session and again briefly the following day, the following week and the following month.

RETENTION OF INFORMATION

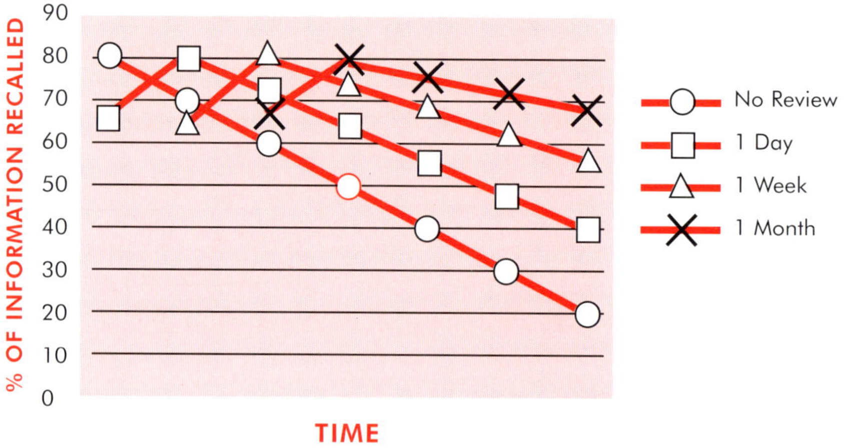


**The more senses we use the more memorable things are.**

Try this way of teaching the 9 planets and their order from the sun. Get the children to act out this scenario, adding plenty of detail, action and sounds. In the center is the **SUN** (e.g. use arms to draw circle in the air). Next to the sun we place a thermometer. It is so hot that the **MERCURY** rises to the top (mime rising mercury) and a blob spills out. A beautiful lady (**VENUS** - the goddess of love) picks up the blob of mercury and throws it (do mime). It lands on **EARTH** (PLOP!) in your back garden where you are sitting eating a **MARS** bar. A man approaches whose hair forms a calf-lick in the shape of a J (for **JUPITER**) on his forehead. He is wearing a T Shirt which has the letters "S" "U" and "N" on it (**SATURN URANUS & NEPTUNE**). He is followed by a small dog – it's the cartoon character **PLUTO**.

# MEMORY STRATEGIES

Teaching strategies which strengthen the neural connections in a child's brain will effectively store skills and information in long term memory. Making these strategies explicit will give pupils the skills they need to create their own excellent memories.

We can now understand that practice, repetition and review works because it provides the stimulation to the neurons to increase myelination and train neurotransmitters. Short, frequent sessions are the most efficient way of practising a skill or reviewing key factors. To be effective, practice must be accurate - it is as easy to commit something to memory incorrectly as to do it correctly (e.g. forming letters).

The more connections that are formed in the brain regarding a particular subject, the easier it is to recall that information. Teach children to approach learning from a number of different directions - e.g. through VAK, 7 intelligences and whole brain thinking.

Using role plays, drama and tableaux increases memory in a variety of ways, providing a memorable context for information, and input through VAK as well as adding in humour and other emotions. Try the role play on the opposite page to teach the nine planets.

Visualisation techniques are particularly effective in enhancing memory. Play games like Kim's game or 'I went to market and bought...' encouraging children to make visual images, such as imagining the objects from Kim's game placed around the room, or building up a picture story of the items on a shopping list.

Other memory strategies include techniques such as using mnemonics, chanting or drawing concept maps. Encourage children to discover what works best for them.

Review and experiment with the 10 memory tips set out on pages 96-97.

# MEMORY – EFFECTIVE RETENTION & RECALL

## Implications for Classroom Practice

| The Implications for Classroom Practice | What to do next |
| --- | --- |
| Learning must be retained in long term memory and be easily recalled if it is to be of benefit | Clearly identify and focus on the skills and knowledge that the lesson seeks to transfer to long term memory |
| The capacity of short term memory is limited to 5 to 9 data items | Present information in small chunks. Use short sentences in both speech and writing |
| If information is not reviewed up to 80% will be lost | Ensure key information is reviewed during lesson, next day, week, month |
| The brain has several different memory systems. The more systems that are used the more information is retained and recalled. | Engage as many of the children's memory systems as possible. Get them to say, hear, see, read and act out what is being learnt |
| The brain remembers well information that has a high emotional content. | Engage the children's emotions, particularly humour during the lesson |
| Information that is stored using both hemispheres is retained and recalled more effectively | Use music, rhythm, rhyme and concept maps to activate both hemispheres |
| Information that is given meaning or associated with existing knowledge is retained and recalled more effectively | Allow children to construct meaning around key facts and associate with known facts |
| Strategies for retaining and recalling information can be learned | Teach memory strategies. |

# ACTION PLAN

What important issues has this chapter raised for you?

What implications does this have for teaching and learning in the classroom?

What implications does this have for teaching and learning at a whole school level?

Proposed Action:

# CHAPTER EIGHT
# THE ROLE OF MOVEMENT IN LEARNING

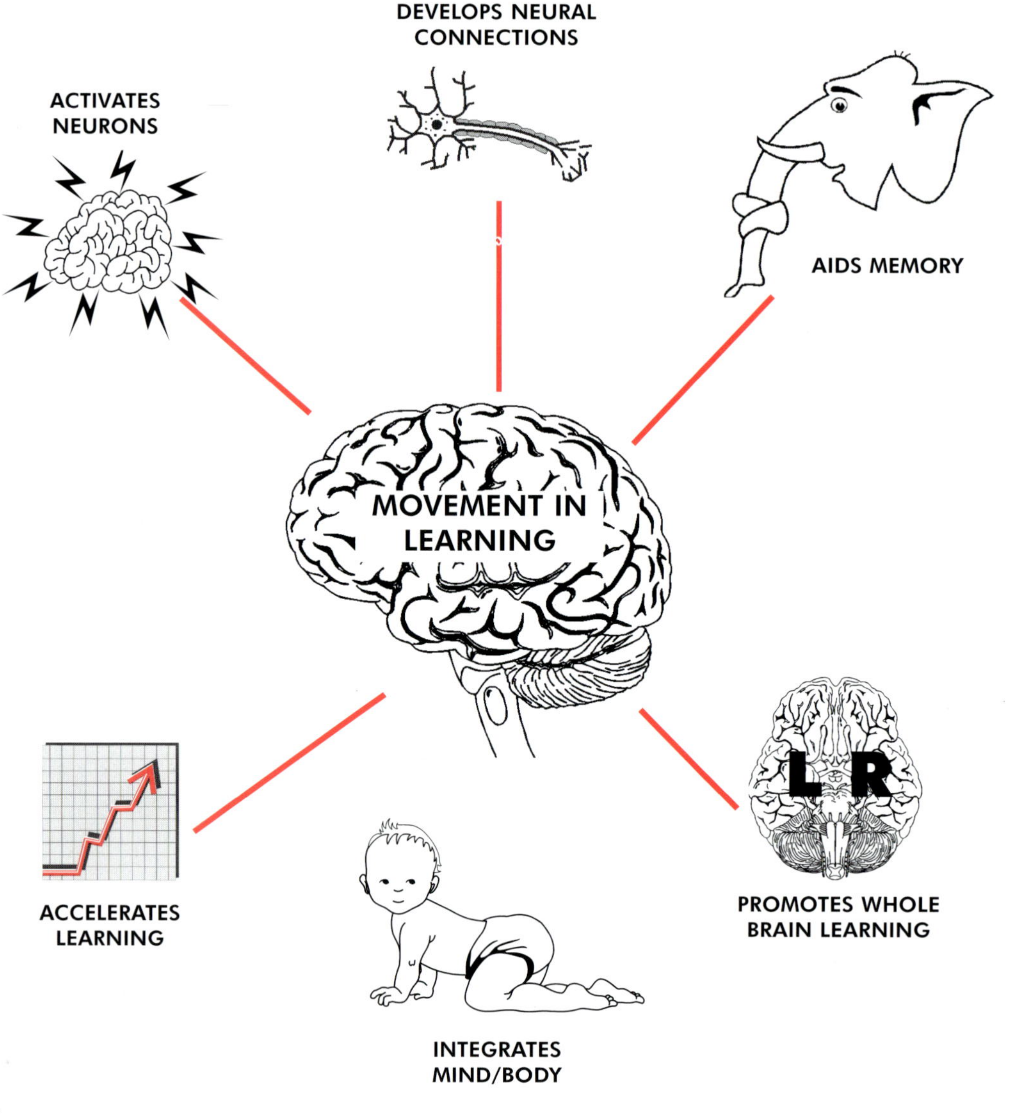

# THE ROLE OF MOVEMENT IN LEARNING

Movement is now recognised as playing an essential part in learning, and building physical activity into the school day is an important part of education.

Scientists now believe that learning takes place not just in the brain, but in the whole body.

### Movement:

- activates the neuron networks;
- stimulates the production of neurotrophins which increase the number of neural connections in the brain;
- aids integration of learning and construction of meaning;
- allows full mind/body integration;
- helps to "bed down" information after a learning session;
- encodes new learning in motor memory.

Nowadays there is increasing acceptance that the human mind/body is all one system and cannot be separated out into purely mental and physical aspects. From the moment of birth movement plays a crucial role as the baby learns to operate successfully in its environment. This role is no less important when the young child starts school.

Research has found exercise programmes to be linked to improved academic performance. However, children today experience an increasingly sedentary lifestyle outside school which makes the issue even more important during the school day.

Kinesiology - the science of motion - has been applied specifically to the field of education by some practitioners. Educational kinesiology offers benefits for all learners, and especially for those who have special needs. Exercises designed to promote whole brain integration are simple and quick to perform, even in a limited space. Try these with your class. Almost invariably those with learning difficulties will have problems performing them at first, but soon get the hang of it.

My class looks forward to our MPE session at registration - it gets the day off to a good start.
Children find the MPE exercises really enjoyable - it puts everyone in a good mood.
I'm keen to develop more of my brain's potential so I use MPE myself.
I use MPE in the dinner queue and after a wet playtime.

# MENTAL/PHYSICAL EXERCISE (MPE)

## 1. Hands and Knees

This exercise gives cross lateral stimulation similar to that obtained by crawling. A characteristic of some children with learning difficulties is that they missed out on the crawling stage as babies.

Raise one knee, and bring the opposite hand to touch it. Repeat with the other hand and knee.

This exercise can be accompanied by counting forwards and backwards, in odd and even numbers, while chanting times tables, etc, killing two birds with one stone! Or play some rousing music as an accompaniment for a complete break state.

## 2. Sky Writing

Have the children write their name in the air with their dominant hand. Then using the other hand, write their name in mirror writing. Finally, use both hands together, writing symmetrically.

Try this yourself.

Which is easier, Stage 2 or Stage 3?

Try using both printing and cursive writing - which is easier?

## 3. Infinity Exercise

Have the children hold a thumb in the air and focus their eyes on their thumb nail. Keeping their eyes on their thumb, they trace an infinity sign in front of them. Swap hands and use the other thumb, then do both together.

# ALPHABET EDIT

| | | | | |
|---|---|---|---|---|
| A | B | C | D | E |
| | | | | |
| F | G | H | I | J |
| | | | | |
| K | L | M | N | O |
| | r | | | |
| | | | | |
| P | Q | R | S | T |
| | | l | | t |
| U | V | W | X | Y |
| | | | | |

Under each letter of the alphabet, write the letter r, l, or t at random with the exception of the following rules.

Rules: an r goes under the L, an l goes under the R, a t goes under the T. No more than three letters the same in any horizontal or vertical line.

Now say the letter of the alphabet out loud, accompanied by the appropriate action.

r = raise right hand   l = raise left hand   t = raise both hands

If you make a mistake, say "whoops" and start again at the beginning. Go through the alphabet in any way you like - forwards, backwards, up and down vertical columns etc.

When you're ready for the next level, add in the opposite foot.

r = raise right hand and left foot   l = raise left hand and right foot
t = raise both hands, and either jump or squat with both knees slightly bent.

Keep changing the sequence of letters underneath the alphabet.

### 4. Macramé Arms

This exercise is good for keeping hands out of mischief while you speak to the children, or for calming down a heated situation.

Hold out arms straight in front and cross them over. Turn palms inwards so they face each other and clasp fingers. Bring hands towards body and up, finishing under your chin.

### 5. Deep Breathing

Encourage children to breathe in from deep in their stomachs, taking in plenty of oxygen to fuel their brains. Try synchronising everyone's breathing for a really calming state.

### 6. Invent your Own!

There are many ideas, such as patting your head and rubbing your stomach at the same time. A good cure for hiccups too!

These exercises take little time, and require little space to do them. Make them part of your daily routine, and use them in the dinner queue, waiting for assembly or in any other situation where you need to maintain control.

# THE ROLE OF MOVEMENT IN LEARNING
## Implications for Classroom Practice

| The Implications for Teaching | What to do next |
|---|---|
| Movement plays an important role in the learning process. | Review practice - assess where movement can fit in to your teaching plans. |
| The human mind/body is all one system and physical and mental aspects cannot be separated. | Adopt a holistic approach to children which recognises the need for both physical and mental stimulation. |
| Certain types of movement (MPE) may help those who have special needs and are beneficial to all children and adults. | Teach MPE to your class and use on a regular basis every day. |
| Children with a kinesthetic learning style have a particularly strong need for movement to be built in to the learning situation. | Assess where it is possible to give highly kinesthetic children opportunities for movement built into lessons. |
| Movement such as MPE can be a useful break-state to recapture concentration. | Use MPE to break up lessons to maintain high levels of concentration. |
| Movement helps to bed down new learning | Offer a period of movement between learning sessions. |

# ACTION PLAN

What important issues has this chapter raised for you?

What implications does this have for teaching and learning in the classroom?

What implications does this have for teaching and learning at a whole school level?

Proposed Action:

# CHAPTER NINE
# THE ROLE OF MUSIC IN LEARNING

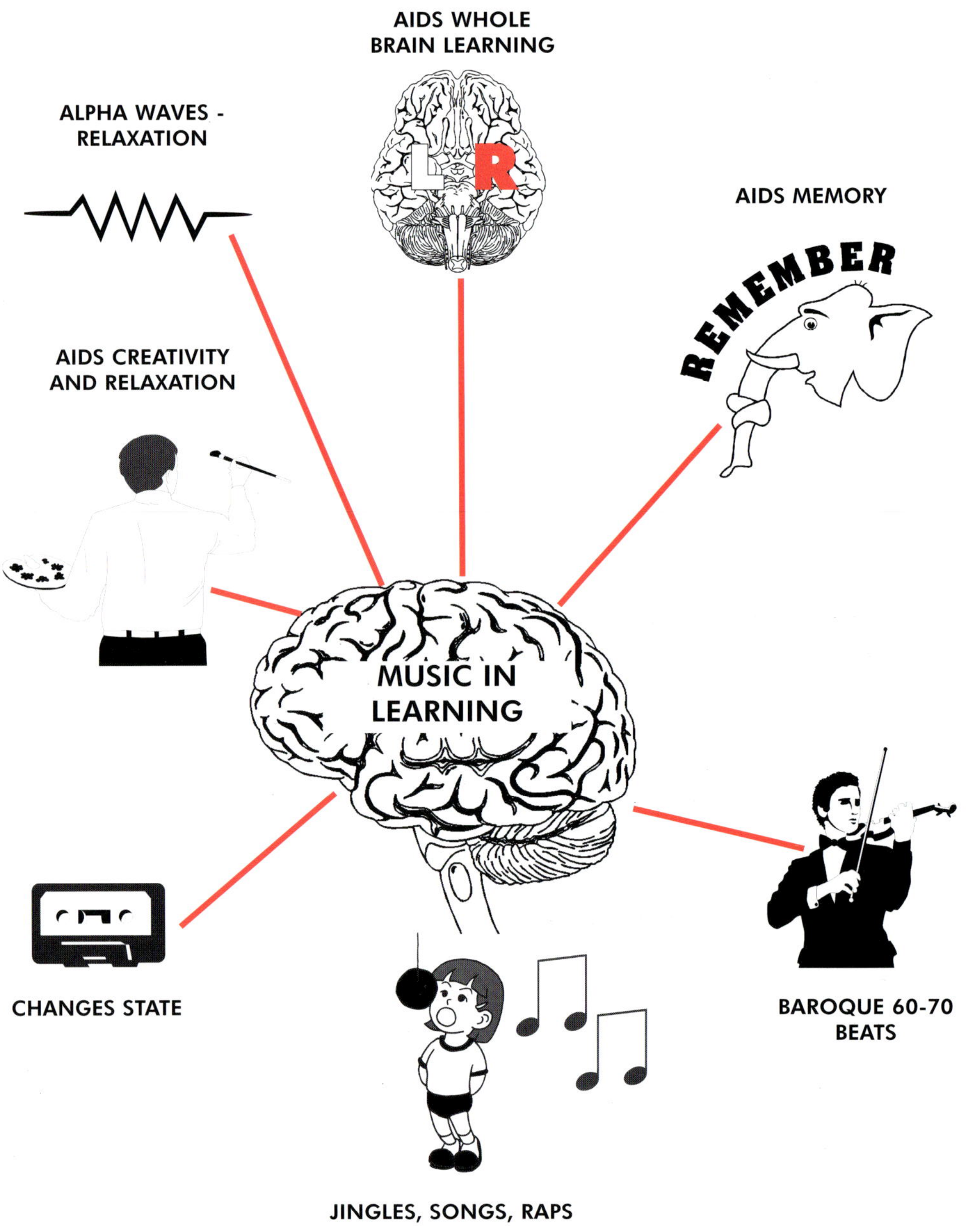

## THE ROLE OF MUSIC IN LEARNING

Music is a powerful aid to learning. It can be used to create an optimal learning state and to boost attention and memory.

Music has been discovered to have some very useful effects. These include:

- significant reductions in the amount of time taken to learn information;
- an actual increase in IQ for the duration of listening to a piece;
- an increase in the level of alpha waves in the brain, thought to be conducive to learning;
- "recharging" the brain cells with electricity, thus energising the brain;
- helping children to focus on an activity, such as art, resulting in reduced noise levels in the classroom;
- stimulating the limbic system, improving encoding in long term memory;
- enhancing relaxation and therefore reducing stress;
- improving whole brain activity by stimulating the right hemisphere;
- increasing creativity and imaginative thinking through brain wave activity.

The type of music you use will depend on the situation and the state you wish to create. See suggestions overleaf.

It is known that music of 60 - 70 beats per minute is especially effective, particularly Baroque music - composers such as Handel, Bach and Mozart. The use of music in the classroom has many applications, from background music as an aid to classroom discipline, to more specific situations.

# SUGGESTIONS FOR MUSIC

## Background: (for raising intelligence levels and reducing noise levels)

| | |
|---|---|
| Mozart | Sonata for Two Pianos in D Major K448 |
| JS Bach | Air on a G string |
| Pachelbel | Canon in D Major |
| Beethoven | Concerto for Violin and Orchestra in D Major op.61 |
| Brahms | Concerto for Violin and Orchestra in D Major op. 77 |

## Guided visualisation: (stimulating alpha waves and unconscious learning)

| | |
|---|---|
| Enya | Memory of Trees |
| Beethoven | Symphony No.6 |
| Mendelssohn | Violin concerto No.1 |
| Handel | Water Music |

## Break States: (energising)

| | |
|---|---|
| Los Lobos | Labamba |
| | Can Can |
| Rossini | William Tell Overture |
| Beethoven | Ode to Joy |

## Goal Setting: (motivation)

| | |
|---|---|
| Vangelis | Chariots of Fire |
| Handel | Hallelujah Chorus |
| Tina Turner | Simply the Best |
| Queen | We are the Champions |

## Relaxation: (stress relief, change of state)

| | |
|---|---|
| L'Esprit | Far Island |
| Handel | Concerto for Harp in F Major Larghetto op.4 no.6 |

Atmospheric music such as Enya

## Concert Review: (played while reviewing material for increased retention)

| | |
|---|---|
| Mozart | Concerto No.21 in C Major, K.467 |
| JS Bach | Fantasy in C Minor |
| Vivaldi | Four Seasons |
| Beethoven | Symphony No.6 |

## WAYS OF USING MUSIC:

Introducing new information - give input against a background of music, matching your voice to fit the rhythm of the music, fading out during active parts and using softer places to speak.

It is important to familiarise yourself with the music and with the content you wish to put over before you try this in the classroom. Allow the music to play for 30 seconds or so before you begin.

Reviewing information - sometimes you might prefer to go over material at the end of the session, speaking to some relaxing music as you recap on information given. Encourage the children to relax and perhaps close their eyes.

Create music to learn specific things, eg, make up little songs including the spelling of a common word:

I s - a - w a bird
I s - a - w a bird
I s - a - w a bird
It sat upon a tree

(Continue with other animals.)

Play background music to keep noise levels down in unstructured activities. However, playing music all day may reduce its impact, so consider introducing it for a third of the teaching day.

# THE ROLE OF MUSIC IN LEARNING

## Implications for Classroom Practice

| The Implications for Teaching | What to do next |
|---|---|
| Certain types of music can boost intelligence and aid concentration during listening. | Build up a bank of suitable tapes/CD's in the classroom. |
| Use of music for up to a third of the teaching day produces benefits. | Plan effective use of music into your daily/weekly plans. |
| Music can help to increase learning at an unconscious level when combined with other techniques. | Plan use of music to enhance relaxation, guided visualisation, review, goal setting, energising etc. |
| Singing/making music is an effective way of getting information into long term memory. | Encourage children to make up songs, jingles and raps to help memorise material. |
| Music stimulates whole brain thinking and useful brain wave frequencies. | Consider when to use music in learning sessions. |

# ACTION PLAN

What important issues has this chapter raised for you?

What implications does this have for teaching and learning in the classroom?

What implications does this have for teaching and learning at a whole school level?

Proposed Action:

# CHAPTER TEN TEACHER TALK

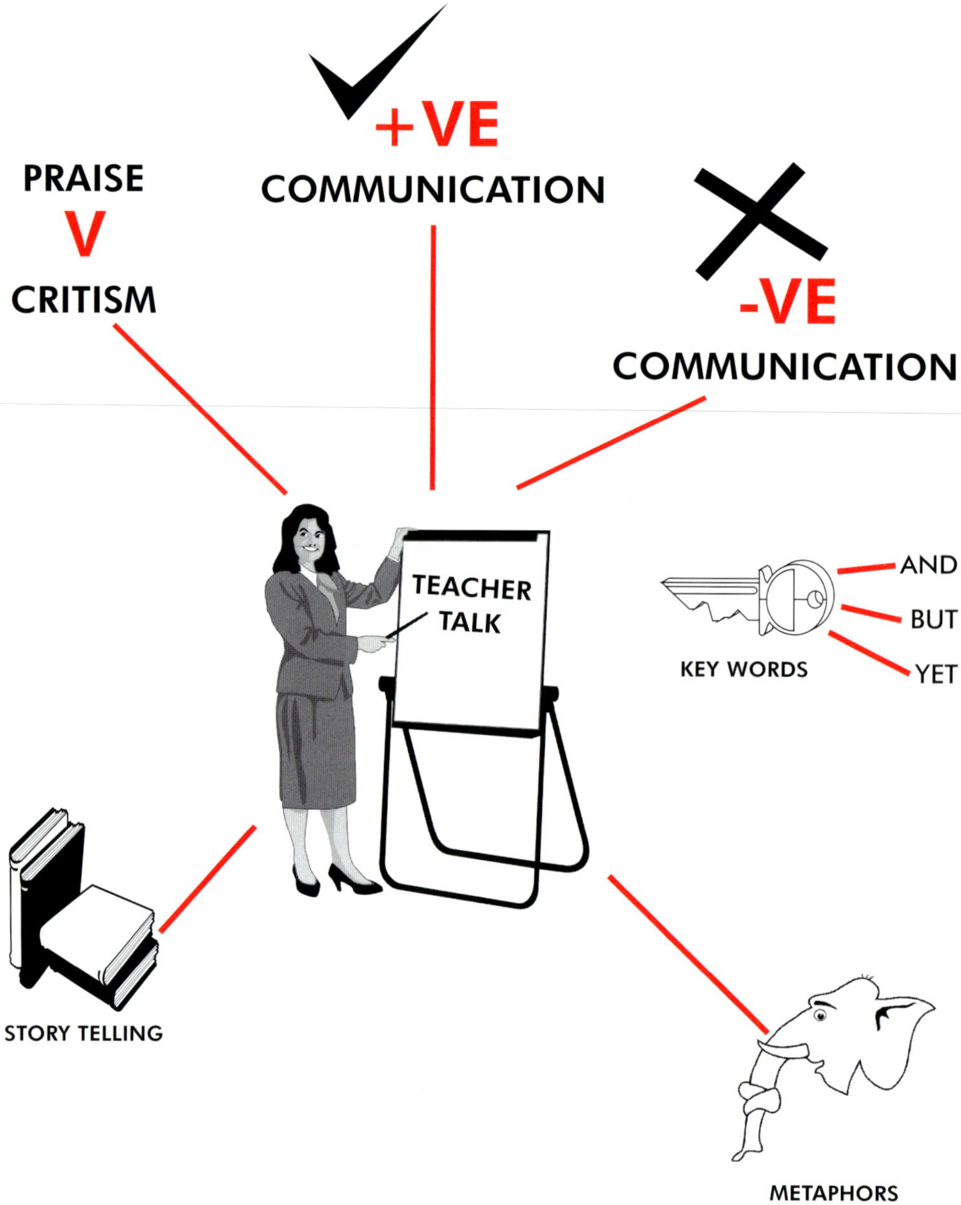

# THE USE OF LANGUAGE IN THE CLASSROOM

The use of language has much potential as a teaching tool. In human communications, language influences us at both conscious and unconscious levels.

Appropriate choice of language can improve learning, influence behaviour and change state.

Adopting certain habits of speech can improve the effectiveness of your communication:-

## Suggestion:

Before you speak, think about the effect you want to achieve and state it in the positive - e.g. "carry that carefully" rather than "don't spill that".

The unconscious mind does not deal in negatives (try NOT to think about a pink elephant...). Any communication framed in the negative, is likely to have the opposite to the desired effect. This is known as an embedded command - the actual message, which may not be the same as the intended one.

Once you are aware of embedded commands in your speech you can use them to your advantage to give messages that are reinforced at unconscious as well as conscious levels.

## Praise v. Criticism

Praise is much more effective than criticism, because use of praise models out good behaviour in the classroom, avoiding a stream of negative embedded commands.

Look for appropriate behaviour and praise it audibly - that way you are sending positive messages at an unconscious level to the whole class, not just an individual. The suggested ratio is 5:1, praise to criticism.

If a child is misbehaving try praising their neighbour(s), and refrain from commenting directly until you can catch them doing something right.

Working in an atmosphere where praise rather than criticism is the order of the day will raise everyone's self-esteem.

## "TEACHER TALK"

### Examples of Positive Communication

"You must feel really proud of this piece of work" *(feel proud)*

"After you worked so hard in last week's lesson you may be surprised at how much easier you find these sums today" *(Find sums easier)*

"When you go home this afternoon, I want you to tell someone about all the things you have achieved today."*(You have achieved things today)*

"Please put this book on the shelf as you go over to tidy your table." *(You are going to tidy your table)*

"What a brilliant story, and when you have gone through and put in the full stops and capital letters it will be superb" *(You have written a brilliant story and are about to make it even better by adding full stops and capitals)*

### How NOT to communicate - or how to communicate the opposite of your intention.

Teacher applying first aid:

> "You'll have to be brave because this is GOING TO REALLY HURT" (Better to say: *"You'll soon forget all about this when you get back to class"*).

Teacher to pupil:

> "Don't PASS THE GLUE OVER KATY'S HEAD - you might SPILL IT ON HER" (Better to say: *"Keep the glue on the table when you pass it"*).
>
> "Andy! If you LEAN BACK ON YOUR CHAIR like that you might FALL" (Better to say: *"Keep all 4 chair legs on the floor and stay safe"*).
>
> Don't WALK ON THE GRASS (Better to say: *"Keep to the concrete path"*).

# THE USE OF LANGUAGE

## 'And' and 'But':

The simple conjunction 'and' is a powerful word. It helps to make your communication positive, especially when giving feedback.

The use of the word 'but' tends to negate what went before it (and sometimes this too can be useful).

In offering feedback,

> 'Well done, you got all your sums right, but your work is very messy' takes something away from the achievement, whereas
>
> 'Well done, you got all your sums right and next time you'll be able to work on your presentation as well' gives a much more positive message as well as setting goals.

## 'Yet'

Another simple word that can transform the effect of a statement. Add it on to the end of any sentence that starts with 'I can't . . .'

## Presuppositions

We unconsciously reveal our expectations by the presuppositions of what we say - that is whatever has to be true in order for our words to make sense. Communication is enhanced if our presuppositions convey positive expectations.

e.g. "Those who finish their work may play with the construction kit" presupposes that some people may not finish their work. The possibility of not finishing is built in.

Whereas..."As soon as you finish your work you may play with the construction kit" ...presupposes that the work will be finished. The expectation of finishing is built in.

## THE POWER OF METAPHOR - THE ELEPHANT STORY

I was driving home from school one evening last June when I got stuck in a traffic jam caused by a convoy of circus lorries turning right into a large field. My eye was caught by a trailer containing two beautiful African elephants. Back home, my children were excited to learn that my late arrival had been caused by the circus and that it was being set up less than a mile way.

On the way home next evening I saw that the circus box office had opened and, as a treat for the family, bought tickets for the opening night. The children were thrilled at the prospect and were full of questions about what they would see. I described some typical circus acts. The thing I could say with certainty was that there would be an elephant act and I told the children about the two elephants I had seen being trained. Melanie, our youngest, was particularly excited about the thought of seeing them.

Our visit to the circus was wonderful. The atmosphere in the big top was electric. A Master of Ceremonies, resplendent in top hat and tails, introduced a series of amazing acts which included jugglers, acrobats, trapeze artists, a lion tamer, clowns and, of course the elephants. It was amazing to see two large and powerful elephants performing graceful balancing acts in the ring. Melanie was enthralled. During the act she asked me why the elephants each had a strong metal ring around their right rear leg. I guessed it was to do with securing them so they couldn't take off.

After the show we walked round the site and Melanie was excited to discover the area where the elephants were. Their trainer was there feeding them some biscuits and fruit. To our delight he invited us over and let us feed them. Melanie pointed out to me that each elephant now had attached to the ring around its rear leg a much lighter chain that was fastened to a small wooden peg that had been tapped into the earth. Melanie asked why, as the elephant was a powerful and strong animal, it didn't break the chain or pull the wooden peg out of the ground.

The trainer heard Melanie's question and answered "For the first part of its life we put a really strong chain on the ring around its leg and attach that chain to a very large rock or a wall. The elephant learns as a baby that its movement is restricted and stops trying to escape. When it grows into an adult it still believes that it cannot move beyond the length of the chain, and limits its own movements accordingly."

## STORY-TELLING AND METAPHOR

Story-telling and the use of metaphor provide a useful tool in the classroom, communicating with pupils at a conscious and non-conscious level.

Story-telling is one of the oldest forms of teaching - the way information was handed down generations before the use of printing was widespread. It is a brain-friendly way of learning. Stories engage emotions, they offer multi-level communication and they can elicit useful states for learning.

Stories are a useful way of starting a session.

They:

- captivate everyone's attention;
- are particularly appealing to right brain dominant learners;
- communicate with the conscious and unconscious mind;
- help to produce optimal learning states;
- promote long-term memory of material;
- motivate pupils.

Metaphors are a particular form of story which promote useful learning at an unconscious level, using circumstances apparently unconnected with the here and now but in which a parallel idea exists. Animals with human characteristics are a popular form of metaphor - Æsop's fables, for example. The conscious mind is distracted by the content of the story, while the intended message is received at a deeper level.

The use of metaphors can be particularly powerful for dealing with issues concerning the emotional intelligences. Stories can be tailor-made to reflect the circumstances and characteristics of the class in order to influence understanding and behaviour.

# TEACHER TALK

## Implications for Classroom Practice

| The Implications for Teaching | What to do next |
|---|---|
| Language can influence at many levels. | Become aware of the power of the language you use and the messages you are sending. |
| The unconscious mind does not recognise negatives. | Say what you do want, not what you don't. |
| 'Embedded commands' sometimes carry messages that are the opposite of what we intend. | Be aware of embedded commands and ensure they are appropriate. |
| Some words like **and** and **yet** are very powerful. | Use language to make communication powerful. |
| The presuppositions of our language reveal expectations and assumptions. | Use presuppositions to convey high expectations. |
| Praise achieves more than criticism. | Identify and praise desirable behaviour. Offer praise unconditionally. |
| Story telling and metaphors are powerful ways to communicate at unconscious levels. | Design stories and metaphors which help to achieve your goals. |

# ACTION PLAN

What important issues has this chapter raised for you?

What implications does this have for teaching and learning in the classroom?

What implications does this have for teaching and learning at a whole school level?

Proposed Action:

# OPTIMAL LEARNING – PUTTING IT ALL TOGETHER

In the preceding chapters, material from a variety of sources has been presented, with the aim of identifying brain compatible teaching methods and techniques in order to produce an optimal learning experience for each child.

In drawing this material together we offer a 10 step Optimal Learning Cycle to assist in planning and delivering lessons for maximum effectiveness.

## 1. Establish an Appropriate Learning Environment.

Take all possible steps to ensure children's physical and emotional well-being. Pupils need to feel safe and secure and have a sense of belonging. They need to have high self-esteem and a strong belief in themselves as learners. They need to have a positive feeling about the learning opportunities they are about to face, know that they will be challenged and that they will succeed.

## 2. Connect the Learning.

Learning is most effective when the student is able to connect what is being learned today with knowledge and understanding that has previously been developed. Brain compatible teaching includes starting lessons by reviewing ground that has been previously covered and explaining how new material builds on this.

## 3. Paint the Big Picture.

Learners, particularly those who favour their right hemisphere, will benefit from the whole lesson being outlined at the beginning – a bit like being shown the lid of a jigsaw before starting to assemble the puzzle.

## 4. Define the Learning Objectives.

It is important that the teacher has clearly defined learning objectives for the session and shares these with the pupils. Ensure that pupils are motivated to learn by explaining **W**hat's **I**n **I**t **f**or **me** and **C**onnecting **I**nto **T**heir **V**alues.

### 5. Present Information.

Research shows that we each have our personal style of learning. Present information in a way that reaches a variety of learning styles so that there is something for everyone. Providing information which is relevant, interesting and has an emotional content will ensure it is more memorable. Remember that the neo-cortex works best in short bursts of concentration.

### 6. Increase Knowledge and Understanding.

To turn knowledge into understanding, pupils need to construct their own meaning from the information they receive. An appropriate activity will allow this opportunity - especially if it encourages pupils to process information through one of the seven intelligences.

### 7. Demonstrating Knowledge and Understanding.

Ultimately students will be required to show what they know. Explaining a concept to a peer or adult is one powerful way of consolidating learning. Providing opportunities for assessment through different intelligences raises self-esteem for children with strengths in areas other than the linguistic or logical mathematical.

### 8. Reviewing for Recall and Retention.

Review is a vital part of ensuring that knowledge and understanding are transferred to long term memory. A regular review cycle will increase recall and retention.

### 9. Feedback.

Regular and immediate feedback dramatically improves learning. Build in feedback mechanisms which include self and peer evaluation. Encourage students to recognise and celebrate reaching goals and targets and to share effective learning strategies with each other.

### 10. Preview.

The speed at which new concepts are learnt can be increased if they are previewed in advance. Teachers could usefully spend the first lesson of each year previewing the whole year's curriculum and the last few minutes of each lesson previewing the next.

## LESSON PLANNING

Date: Class: Position in Lesson Sequence:
Learning Objective:

**Introduction:** **Time:**

Build self esteem.
Give Big Picture
Connect to previous learning
Remember WIIfm & CITV
Build learning state

**Input:** **Time:**

Delivery through: L/R & Whole Brain

V A K

**Activity – constructing meaning:** **Time:**

Tick as appropriate

V A K

Linguistic Math/logic Visual/spatial
Kinesthetic

Musical Interpersonal Intrapersonal

**Review:** **Time:**

**Preview:** **Time:**

# A CLASS ACT

## ACQUIRING AND ABSORBING INFORMATION

A

- Create brain compatible learning environment
- Build state of high self esteem and relaxed alertness
- Connect to previous learning
- Engage attention (RAS) – remember WIIfm and CITV
- Construct strong positive self image as learners
- Define and share learning objectives
- Deliver in short bursts and access both hemispheres
- Deliver through VAK, take account of learning styles
- Build good learning states like curiosity and anticipation

## CONSTRUCTING MEANING

C

- Provide activities which construct & consolidate understanding
- Offer opportunities to use different intelligences
- Give regular feedback and build in peer and self assessment
- Engage interest through relevant and stimulating activities
- Use music and other techniques to encourage non-conscious learning
- Build in opportunities for movement
- Discuss and share learning strategies

## TRANSFERRING TO & TRIGGERING MEMORY

T

- Identify skills and knowledge to be transferred to memory
- Appeal to emotions, particularly humour
- Encourage the use of different memory systems
- Review skill and key information regularly
- Test for retention and feedback
- Teach and use memory strategies

## HEMISPHERE DOMINANCE QUESTIONNAIRE

Carefully read the following 12 pairs of statements and quickly decide, by ringing the appropriate letter, whether statement a) or statement b) is the better description of you.

**1. If you were doing a jigsaw puzzle would you be more likely to:**

a) sort all the pieces into categories (eg corners, straight edges, sky, bits of cars etc)?

b) begin by sorting the edges and corners but fit bits together as you spot them?

**2. Which box would you more readily pair with box 1:**

a) box 2?

b) box 3?

**3. When you buy a new appliance (eg video recorder, microwave oven etc) would you be more likely to:**

a) briefly examine the instruction booklet and experiment?

b) carefully read and follow the instructions?

**4. If you were going on holiday would you prefer to:**

a) plan what you are doing well in advance?

b) book at the last minute and perhaps get a bargain?

**5. Do you have hunches about the future or how things will turn out:**

a) fairly often?

b) hardly ever?

**6. When you are writing a letter, typing a report, designing a work sheet etc, do you:**

a) regularly check your work/carefully read what you have written or typed?

b) find checking your work a bit of a chore?

**7 Is your work area:**

a) usually organised and you can locate papers and items easily?

b) regularly requires you to search through a "muddle" for a report or item?

**8. When you are given a task with a deadline do you:**

a) usually plan in advance and beat the deadline?

b) only really get stuck in as the deadline looms large?

**9. Which box would you more readily pair with box 1:**

a) box 2?

b) box 3?

**10. When faced with a problem would you say you tend to:**

a) get a feel for the situation and possible solutions?

b) gather and analyse the facts so that you understand the situation better?

**11. When you are tackling a project are you more likely to:**

a) make a few notes to start with?

b) establish an outline and structure the main issues, themes and tasks?

**12. Do you prefer to:**

a) read the book and then decide whether you will see the film?

b) see the film?

Give yourself 1 point each time you:

answered a) to the following questions: 2, 3, 5, 10 and 11.

answered b) to the following questions: 1, 4, 6, 7, 8, 9 and 12.

Now mark your score on the continuum below.

**L** 0 1 2 3 4 5 6 7 8 9 10 11 12 **R**

# MULTIPLE INTELLIGENCE PROFILE

Scoring: Carefully read each statement and then quickly assess on a scale of 0 to 5 how well the statement describes you, scoring yourself "5" if you strongly agree with the statement and "0" if you strongly disagree. Write your score for each statement on the right. Add up your score for each section. Enter your score in the appropriate column overleaf.

## Section A

I find it easy to express myself in writing. ...3...
I find it easy to follow a lecture or written article. ...4...
I have a large vocabulary. ...2...
I am good at explaining things to others. ...4...
Total ...13...

## Section B

I have a feeling for working with numbers ...4...
I am good at picking out patterns. ...1...
I enjoy problem solving. ...1...
I like to work through a task in a logical, orderly manner. ...4...
Total ...10...

## Section C

I am good at map reading. ...1...
I find it easy to do puzzles which involve rotating shapes. ...1...
I can hold an image in my mind. ...4...
I find graphs & diagrams helpful in understanding information. ...3...
Total ...9...

## Section D

I can remember a tune easily. ...1...
I can play a musical instrument. ...0...
I can easily pick out different instruments playing in an orchestral piece. ...0...
I enjoy spending time listening to or making music. ...4...
Total ...5...

## Section E

I like working with my hands. ...3...
I find it difficult to sit still for long. ...3...
I enjoy physical activity and have good co-ordination. ...2...
I prefer hands on learning activities to reading or listening. ...2...
Total ...10...

## Section F

I work well in a team. ...4...
I have a lot of empathy with others. ...4...
I enjoy mixing with other people. ...5...
I am good at talking people into things ...4...
Total ...17...

## Section G

I am self motivated. ...4...
I am good at controlling my moods. ...4...
I can work well in a team but work even better on my own. ...4...
I am aware of my own behaviour and how it affects others. ...4...
Total ...16...

# YOUR RELATIVE INTELLIGENCE ASSESSMENT

| SECTION A | SECTION B | SECTION C | SECTION C | SECTION E | SECTION F | SECTION G |
|---|---|---|---|---|---|---|
| 20 | 20 | 20 | 20 | 20 | 20 | 20 |
| 19 | 19 | 19 | 19 | 19 | 19 | 19 |
| 18 | 18 | 18 | 18 | 18 | 18 | 18 |
| 17 | 17 | 17 | 17 | 17 | 17 | 17 |
| 16 | 16 | 16 | 16 | 16 | 16 | 16 |
| 15 | 15 | 15 | 15 | 15 | 15 | 15 |
| 14 | 14 | 14 | 14 | 14 | 14 | 14 |
| 13 | 13 | 13 | 13 | 13 | 13 | 13 |
| 12 | 12 | 12 | 12 | 12 | 12 | 12 |
| 11 | 11 | 11 | 11 | 11 | 11 | 11 |
| 10 | 10 | 10 | 10 | 10 | 10 | 10 |
| 9 | 9 | 9 | 9 | 9 | 9 | 9 |
| 8 | 8 | 8 | 8 | 8 | 8 | 8 |
| 7 | 7 | 7 | 7 | 7 | 7 | 7 |
| 6 | 6 | 6 | 6 | 6 | 6 | 6 |
| 5 | 5 | 5 | 5 | 5 | 5 | 5 |
| 4 | 4 | 4 | 4 | 4 | 4 | 4 |
| 3 | 3 | 3 | 3 | 3 | 3 | 3 |
| 2 | 2 | 2 | 2 | 2 | 2 | 2 |
| 1 | 1 | 1 | 1 | 1 | 1 | 1 |
| Linguistic Intelligence | Mathematical/ Logical Intelligence | Visual/Spatial Intelligence | Musical Intelligence | Bodily Kinesthetic Intelligence | INTER Personal Intelligence | INTRA Personal Intelligence |

# TRAINING AND CONSULTANCY ON OPTIMAL LEARNING

This book is based on a highly successful one day course "Optimal Learning in the Primary Classroom" run by Sara Shaw and Trevor Hawes.

A high percentage of teachers describe this day as *"the best one day's training they have ever had", "inspirational" and "highly informative and fun"*

An impressive feature of the day is that Sara and Trevor practise what they preach – consistently creating the conditions and using the techniques that research has proven maximises the quality and quantity of learning.

For details of how this course could be run in your area for a group of schools or as an INSET day at your school contact the authors on:


| | |
|---|---|
| Telephone: | 0116 2717217 |
| FAX: | 0116 2717219 |
| Write to: | Optimal Learning PO Box 12<br>Leicester LE2 5AE, England |
| Email: | THESERVICES@COMPUSERVE.COM |